Deep Into My Eyes

From Victim to Vegas Headliner

Kevin Lepine

Biography & Autobiography / Entertainment & Performing Arts

Deep Into My Eyes

From Victim to Vegas Headliner

Las Vegas, NV USA
www.HypnosisUnleashed.com

Cover Design by: Olayemi Bolaji
Editing by: Marti McKenna & Bridget McKenna
Kevin's Headshot by: Jimi Robinson

Personal Dynamics Publishing
www.PersonalDynamicsPublishing.com

ISBN: 979-8-9888867-1-6

Author's Note: *This book is not intended to provide medical or mental health advice, diagnosis, or treatment.*

Table of Contents

Preface

The moment I saw this picture on the cover, I knew I had to write my book. The image summed up the message I want to spread to the world. My journey from victim to Vegas headliner starts with isolation and continues with celebration. My story touches on a lot of deep topics including: depression, suicide, abuse, and addiction. I'm not a medical professional. This book is not intended to provide medical or mental health advice, diagnosis, or treatment.

This book also contains the story of my victory overcoming, and growing from those issues. I'm excited for you to learn about how the communities I've built saved me, and gave me the life I always dreamed. I hope this book gives you the strength to do the same!

~ Kevin

Acknowledgements

So many people came together to make this book a reality. Jeff and Meg Zampino, Tobias Beckwith, and Ariana Tobin for being my first copy editors. Michael Johns for going over it with me word by word. Jaq Greenspun for explaining I needed people like that, and Ken Owens for turning it from an abstract idea into a physical book.

My wonderful wife, Emily, whose patience and love has made everything possible.

Everyone I have mentioned in the book, thank you for the love and helping me grow beyond myself. Don't worry, names have been changed to protect the guilty.

Chris M., Brian M., and Darius, who provided some bright moments in very dark times.

To all my family: Lepines, Goldmans, Jedynaks, and Tobins, thank you for all the love and acceptance.

Thank you God, for the grace of getting me this far; let's keep it going!

And to you, yes YOU! Thank you for reading this.

Foreword

In the 1990's, I was very interested in what made people successful. I looked at IQ scores and other measures of aptitude. I came up with the theory that what creates success is drive and the willingness to listen. It couldn't be talent, because we all know very talented people who are not successful, and many untalented people who are. Drive is your ability to get back up when you've been hurt and willingness to listen is your ability to take ideas from either life lessons or other people. I didn't know it at the time, but Elizabeth Duckworth was working on a similar theory with much more detail.

Kevin was one of the people I watched to come up with ideas and they are also part of the keys to Kevin's success. His ability to keep trying to build a community even when he was hurt, and his willingness to consider and test advice from almost anyone to build his skills and work on building his community. If he had not focused on community building, he would not be successful or happy. It is not Gandalf's magical power that defeats Mordor, it's his ability to connect even in the worst of times.

I come to this book from the point of view of a close friend and a licensed professional who has dedicated his life to the helping professions. Like anyone who is interested in people, I've learned a lot from watching those around me. My grandmother always told me about the importance of observing people. It's been clear to me from the first time I met Kevin, that even in his early years, he carried a lot of pain and empathy; and reading the book it is easy to see why. With Kevin, you could always see his empathy lurking. It was always present even when his pain overshadowed it.

One of the things that became clear to me watching Kevin for many years is that he's an incredibly loyal person, sometimes to his detriment. In this book, he talks about building a network of people around him and through his life, and you'll see the theme of loyalty throughout the book, which has always gained him more than it cost him.

I believe that people will be inspired by this book and will see themselves in ways that can be very helpful. It's inspiring to learn that other people have survived dark times and dark places; and now thrive. Others will recognize the pain. Because of that pain, they will have trouble following the advice of the book. If this feels like you when you finish, and you find you still have trouble building your community, you can look for to the following websites for help or your primary care physician.

- www.emdria.org
- https://ifs-institute.com/practitioners
- www.traumahealing.org
- www.bcia.org

***William Arendell*, LCSW**

www.arenhealth.com

Chapter 1

Welcome to the Middle

> ***A brave man once requested me***
>
> ***To answer questions that are key***
>
> ***"Is it to be or not to be?***
>
> ***And I replied, "Oh, why ask me?"*** *~Johnny Mandel*

I was fifteen years old and ready to take my own life. All the abuse and pain had destroyed any chance of my seeing love or hope. The negative voices in my head had become sharks circling for the kill.

We have all had to endure sharks in our lives. Those people who have hunted us, attacked us, and harmed us, sometimes seemingly only for their own pleasure. At that moment of darkness, the sharks had won. I was filled with despair and feeling utterly alone. All the negative, harmful people had worn me down and defeated me. I was drowning. I had no willpower to continue going on the way I had been living with so much pain.

I wish I could reach through time and hug that kid. I wish I could tell him all the things that were ahead of him. That he would live out his dreams. That he would travel the world and experience diverse cultures. If he only knew, one day he would be a headliner in Las Vegas, making people laugh. Mostly, I would tell him about all the love that awaited him. But at that moment, he couldn't see it. He was too young, too naïve, too hurt to see another possibility. He needed a miracle. He didn't know it that night, but a miracle was about to happen.

I have done so much with my life that I want to share with you. I want to share this incredible journey that is still in progress. But to understand all the great things I have achieved, you need to know how I got through that moment of deep despair, and how I found the strength to move past that moment and reach my dreams.

Chapter 2

Everything Begins Somewhere

> ***"Welcome to your life,***
>
> ***There's no turning back."*** *~Tears for Fears*

I am going to tell you the story of Kevin's early years. I must tell you the story of *his* early years because they do not feel like *mine*. Those years filled with so much pain that most of it is a blur. Those years feel like they happened to someone else—someone I knew a long time ago.

You will meet a lot of people throughout this story. You'll encounter flashbacks, flashforwards, and even flash-sideways with them. It seems to me that this is how we experience people in our lives. Sometimes we meet a person, and only years later do we realize how important they are to our story. Other times we meet someone and have an instant connection, never knowing if the moment will be fleeting or forever. I am excited for you to meet all of them. For now, let us start at the beginning.

Kevin's birth parents put him up for adoption when he was five months old. They will play a significant role later in the story. Right now, they were two people far too young to raise a child. He was fortunate to spend only a month in foster care before the adoption agency put him into his mother Rosemary's arms on Christmas Eve 1975.

Rosemary was extremely excited to be a mother. Unable to conceive a child with her then-husband, she was thrilled to receive this Christmas present. She was loud and brassy. She always spoke her mind and never censored her thoughts or actions. Many people would say she wore her emotions on her sleeve. It would be more correct to say she wore her emotions like a coat of many colors. You never had to wonder what she was thinking or feeling.

She did her best to spread friendliness and kindness. Her empathetic ways would bring many people close to her. Sometimes those same emotions were too much for people to handle, and she would push them away. But she always tried to act with love. Loud, brassy, take-no-shit love.

Unfortunately, her marriage was volatile and abusive. Her husband would become one of the first sharks in Kevin's life—a shark that would introduce Kevin to fear and uncertainty. Within 3 years, the marriage would end with Rosemary's ex-husband having visitation rights. A year later, Rosemary would marry Charles Lepine, and a family would truly begin.

Chuck and Rosemary had an unconventional marriage. They had known each other from years before when she'd been a secretary at his insurance agency, and he'd been a drunk. Now years later, they'd reconnected, and he was sober, working as an engineer on the railroad. His work schedule had him gone for days at a time, yet he always found time when home to be very present.

Chuck's sobriety really brought him and Rosemary back together. Being in A.A. brought Chuck not only sobriety but a calmer path than he had been raised on. Chuck's dad had been abusive, and he never wanted to pass that behavior on. While he yelled now and then, he never raised a hand to Kevin in anger. The other thing A.A. gave Chuck was the ability to be honest about himself and his life. He never lied about who he was or what he did. He told Kevin many stories about his drinking life, and while every story was funny, the stories were also tragic. The time he was so drunk he got into the back of a police car thinking it was a cab. When he got so drunk he passed out and slept through the Detroit riots happening 10 floors below his office. He told stories of totaling cars, hurting himself, and of the loneliness that alcoholism brought on. Because Chuck was always honest, Kevin never felt the need to test him or repeat his mistakes.

Chuck and Rosemary always treated Kevin like an adult. They never used childish voices or language around him and gave him the respect they would give to other adults. They constantly nourished his love for reading. He devoured any book he could get his hands on; Sweet Pickles and any other junior reading books the library had, he wanted read to him. He learned letters and was reading by himself before long.

His parents encouraged him to try new things. Sports were not high on his list, as he was a small, underweight child with no coordination and not much balance or control. He didn't even learn to ride a bike until he was about seven. On his first bike ride, not knowing how to stop, he closed his eyes until he crashed into a parking lot wall. Eventually, he got the hang of both riding and stopping safely.

Unfortunately, raising him this way did make him socially awkward. He spoke like an adult. He didn't understand the slang kids used. It was much easier to talk to adults than kids. While he understood when an adult would ask him something directly and clearly, he didn't understand when kids were selfish, and their joking and teasing confused him.

Kindergarten started and the problems began. Rosemary and Chuck, reasoning that it was a better opportunity for Kevin, sent him to a Catholic school. Even early on he had trouble making friends. Teasing hurt. The other kids smelled blood and took every opportunity to ridicule him. They'd gang up on him and mock him until he cried.

His attention span was limited. He could grasp a concept easily and memorize things quickly, but repetitive teaching bored him horribly. He would daydream often; existing in his own world, unaware that the rest of the class had moved on to other activities. He was far more interested in what was going on out the window or in his own imagination than in whatever the teacher was talking about.

Tasks requiring focus and fine motor skills defied him. He found things like coloring in the lines difficult and painful. His handwriting was atrocious. He was left-handed, and the teachers tried to make him write with his right hand to even worse results. They gave up on that and told him being left-handed meant he would never have good handwriting.

His teachers made fun of him when he couldn't do art projects or anything that needed fine motor skills. His brain moved so much faster than his body, and he had almost no control. His kindergarten teacher laughed at him when he couldn't "correctly" color in an American flag. She made him do it over, which only frustrated him and made the coloring worse. Later, Kevin would be diagnosed with A.D.D., but at the time, teachers simply told him to pay better attention.

One thing he did pay attention to was that he was going to have a brother soon! Chuck and Rosemary were having another child. John was born in 1979, and Kevin loved his little brother. He loved John even as the boy grew up troubled. John would be diagnosed with many illnesses throughout his life: schizophrenia, Tourette's, A.D.H.D., psychosis, and more. While the brothers loved each other, it was not an easy childhood for either of them. John battled inner demons every day, and Kevin dealt with the fallout. John had no impulse control and broke anything Kevin had. All John wanted to do was play with his big brothers' things. Unfortunately, to John, playing and breaking were the same thing. There was nothing Kevin could have that John would not find a way to destroy. Kevin's Christmas and birthday presents would be broken within a week. No matter what he did to protect his things, John found them and broke them. None of it was malicious—it was part of John's constant struggle. Because of his brother's challenges, Kevin had to learn about mental illness the hard way. If John wasn't breaking Kevin's things, he was following his big brother around nonstop, constantly trying to force a reaction out of him. John insulted most anyone who came to the house. The mental illness made him lash out in so many ways.

One morning when John was about five, Kevin reached his limit. Only Kevin and John were awake. John broke Kevin's Transformer toy in front of Kevin's face, laughed, and threw it at Kevin. Kevin lost control. He quickly pinned John to the floor, brought his fist back, and was ready to slam it into his brother's face.

Just as the punch was about to land, John said: "I haven't taken my pills yet." But he said it with an uncontrollable, hysterical laughter that was filled with sadness.

Kevin wanted to hit John so badly at that moment. All the built-up frustration was right there waiting to explode. But he knew that if John hadn't taken his meds, he likely wasn't in control of his actions. He could hear the lack of control in John's voice.

Kevin struggled to understand the depths of his brother's mental illness. Almost impossible. But he had been learning alongside Chuck and Rosemary what John's mental illness meant: that John couldn't control a lot of his thoughts and that those thoughts would become instant actions without medication. Kevin just walked away and mourned the loss of yet another thing that was supposed to have been his.

Living with John was like living with the constant threat that a tornado might tear through the house at any moment. Chuck and Rosemary did their best to contain him. Unfortunately, the main thing Kevin learned was that John was able to destroy anything Kevin had with no consequences. While that was not entirely true, it felt true to Kevin most of the time.

A year after John's birth, Chuck and Rosemary gave birth to a baby girl named Colleen, who was kind and funny. Colleen needed a lot of help as well. But with their focus on managing John's issues, they didn't really see Colleen's reading difficulties or Kevin's A.D.D. And Kevin's issues were getting worse with every passing year.

Kevin was still being bullied a lot in school. In addition to the constant ridicule, he was interrupted so often that he developed a stutter. He began to care less and less about himself. He felt so worthless that he stopped caring about his appearance. It was common for him to skip combing his hair or to wear wrinkled clothes he'd picked up off the bedroom floor.

Then the sharks began to circle, and the fights began. Not one kid starting a fight, but groups of kids pushing him, smacking him, beating on him. Even the older kids joined in. Kids would come from every corner to join in on the feeding frenzy. Kevin began to feel like a victim because he was a victim. The more he felt like a victim, the more kids treated him like one.

Anytime he thought he had made a friend, that person would make up stories about him the next week at school. Slowly Kevin retreated inside himself. He would take his bike and go riding by himself for hours.

While his family was not poor, there was not a lot of extra money. Kevin would search for bottles to turn in for change to buy himself sodas or candy while he biked around town. He took on a paper route at age 10 and got a job sweeping and mopping up in a local pharmacy as well.

He read voraciously. If he couldn't have friends, he could read about them. Over time, the characters he read about became more real than people in real life. The characters in the book were kind and offered him stories. The people in real life offered him pain and misery.

Rosemary's first husband still had visitation rights that Kevin wanted no part of. Kevin had never felt close to him. Rosemary's resentment of her former husband made Kevin even more uncomfortable. Maybe the man tried to be there, but Kevin never felt it. Often, he felt dumped at the man's parents' house or in front of the TV. While his grandma and grandpa on the man's side were always loving, Kevin never felt a bond. When he was ten, Rosemary decided on an idea that would sever the bond completely. She convinced Kevin to tell her ex-husband to give up all parental rights and let Chuck adopt him.

Putting that break-up on ten-year-old Kevin's shoulders was a mistake on Rosemary's part. The situation was further complicated by Kevin's fear of making anyone feel hurt or angry. He knew this conversation would make the man feel both. The lead-up was gut-wrenching. The next time Rosemary's ex-husband came to pick him up, Kevin was going to tell the man that he wanted Chuck to adopt him. Rosemary wanted what was best, but she chose the worst way possible. There were more appropriate ways for her to do this. She could have reached out to family courts for assistance. But she didn't have the emotional ability to handle it herself or find the right channels. Still, it never should have fallen on a scared child's shoulders.

But Kevin did it. Shaky and terrified, he asked his legal father to let Chuck adopt him. Then he watched the man walk out the door for the last time. Kevin had one more phone call with the man. The call felt like it went on for hours but was probably less than 15 minutes, with Rosemary prompting him. Again, not a conversation Kevin should have had to have at all. The court could have supplied a safe space. It could have been a group call with everyone. A child terrified of disappointing anyone should never have had to do anything like that.

The upside is that Kevin got what he truly wanted: Chuck adopted him. This was an immense joy. For all the problems outside the house, inside the house his mom and dad were a sanctuary. He loved his siblings dearly. He understood John had problems, and the family worked on those problems the best they could. But external abuse was building up.

Chuck and Rosemary gave Kevin unconditional love. Despite all the pain he experienced outside the home, inside he felt safe. Rosemary was warm, caring, and empathetic. Chuck was straightforward and honest. Kevin never had to question whether something Chuck said was true. Chuck was honest about himself, his past, and being a proud member of Alcoholics Anonymous. This straightforward honesty put Kevin on a path to avoiding drugs and alcohol. He never saw either as an escape— more as something that would impair and distract him. With everything in store for him, this would be a redeeming quality. He was drawn to compulsive behavior; he just did not know it yet.

Once Kevin completed fifth grade, Chuck and Rosemary decided the school was a toxic environment for the kids. They had noticed his stutter and the way he was withdrawing. They saw the sadness he brought home with him every day. There was another catholic school a bit further away that seemed better, with smaller classrooms that would in theory be a better fit for John and Colleen as well.

It was not.

Kevin was in a smaller class. He would later come to believe that feeling like a victim made him an easy target. He was a nerd. Scrawny with glasses, his nose in a book, an object of ridicule. His stutter had increased, and when he did speak, it was to say something spiteful. After years of bullying, he'd lost empathy. He was in pain, angry at everyone, and he'd learned how to verbally give much worse than he got. Confronted with ugly words, he would fire back with the meanest thing he could think of.

This only led to more fights and pain.

John's mouth was out of control. Tourette's Syndrome made him say horrible things to everyone. The other kids did not understand it was not intentional. Kevin tried to defend his brother, which led to more fights and made Kevin even more of an outcast.

In his search for human connection, Kevin joined a scouting troop. He saw Eagle Scouts as a modern knighthood. He was determined to earn what very few ever would: The Eagle Award. While he would thrive in scouting, he would mostly thrive alone. Any friendship made with peers on a campout would shatter come school on Monday.

The school was woefully underfunded. By eighth grade, Kevin mostly learned from his own reading. His entire class failed the high school placement exam because the teacher neglected to prepare them in any way. You have never seen anything funnier or sadder than a nerdy, skinny, stuttering kid walking into class angry after that test.

"I failed that placement," Kevin said with tears in his eyes.

"You don't know that," his teacher replied.

"Then what is the answer to this question?" he said writing the following:

$3 \cdot 2 =$

"Six," she answered.

"Why?"

"Because the dot means to multiply."

"You never taught me ANY of that," he cried, anger and sorrow thick in his voice.

To the teacher's credit, she knew she had let her students down. She sought out better textbooks and taught the class everything they needed to know to pass that exam. When they sat for the test again, Kevin placed in the top three percent of students statewide.

Kevin stopped asking for help with the bullying. The administration had failed him too many times. Whenever a teacher talked about bullying, he'd get another pounding. The administration was almost worse than the bullies. The female principal thought it was her duty to watch the little boys change after gym class, ostensibly to make sure nothing inappropriate was happening.

Obviously, the school was not prepared to deal with the children from the top down.

His teachers did not understand how to help Kevin at all. They tended to ignore him. It was easier to let him sit in a corner and read than to figure him out. They repeatedly passed him up for opportunities in gifted programs, not for his lack of ability, but because he did not fit in socially. Because the "smart kids" picked on him, he was not allowed to be part of their accelerated math or reading groups. Teachers used the other children's abuse as an excuse to deny him opportunities.

One day in eighth grade, Kevin's temper reached a boiling point. Most of the time he could retreat inside himself, but on this day he just couldn't, and his rage finally erupted. He was in a library study group with two other students, and as usual, one of them was picking on him. Kevin began to cry, hard. He begged the other kid to stop, but they would not. Kevin snapped. The last wave of true emotion overrode anything rational in his mind. He would not remember getting up from his chair and getting behind the kid. He would have had no memory of wrapping his hands around the kid's neck. He would only remember repeatedly slamming the kid's head into the table, his hands squeezing the neck of his tormentor, the kid clawing at his hands, while the other kid struggled to pull him off.

Kevin snapped back to reality. He let the kid go, went into the bathroom, locked the door, and cried for the final time. His emotions were burnt out, done. He felt numb to everything.

He could still feel anxiety, and he had a good reason to be anxious. The Lepines were moving to a new town, and Kevin would be going to an all-boys Catholic high school.

Chapter 3

A Place Away from Torment

> ***"Things are gonna get easier,***
>
> ***Ooh child,***
>
> ***Things'll get brighter."*** *~Five Stairsteps*

Reading was a safe space for Kevin. In first grade, he misunderstood his first reading assignment. While the teacher assigned the first story in the semester's storybook, Kevin thought he had to read the whole book. He was glad to do it. Reading opened so many doors in his imagination. He was always reaching for new books. Throughout his school years, he would always read at a higher level than his classmates and read as much as he could.

Throughout the years, reading would become his main passion. Science fiction, science fantasy, Isaac Asimov, Hardy Boys—any escapist reading called to him. He repeatedly devoured *The Outsiders* by S.E. Hinton. *Dragonlance* novels and fantasy characters enthralled him.

And there was something even better than reading for him. He would find love and happiness by telling the story.

In second grade, he was given the chance to do a reading at the church for his class's first communion. The teacher selected him because, while he would stutter when talking around people, when asked to read aloud in class, he was confident. His stutter vanished. She had him read aloud a number of times in class, then offered him the opportunity to read for the church ceremony. Of course, Kevin said yes. While personal speaking was impossible, public speaking was easy.

Reciting material aloud was the simplest of tasks. He instinctively understood the secret to public speaking: The audience was there to hear what he had to say. This was the opposite of his day-to-day life where he felt no one wanted to listen to him. He didn't feel rushed or nervous or unsure of himself. Instead, he felt confident in his ability. He had unknowingly discovered the very thing that would bring him joy and success.

Anytime there was a recital, performance, or anything that involved speaking, Kevin would jump at it. He could not fit in on an interpersonal level, but he found a safe space on every stage. Those stages quickly became his refuge. This was the one place nothing hurt him, a place he felt secure. Not having to think before he spoke, just to recite the words in front of him—it was comforting. Best of all, he received positive attention. No one made fun of him, because no one else wanted what came so easy to him. On stage, he could hold an audience's attention. He felt wanted and validated. He could barely talk to anyone one-on-one, but he could speak to a crowd of hundreds.

Jerry Seinfeld said, "According to most studies, people's number one fear is public speaking. Number two is death. This means to the average person, if you go to a funeral, you're better off in the coffin than doing the eulogy." Not for Kevin. For Kevin, this was a place of true comfort and everywhere *else* felt like a coffin.

His mom even put him in a community play in fourth grade where he was the farmer munchkin in *The Wizard of Oz*. Learning that he could be someone else on stage was a revelation. The more he felt tormented by others, the less he liked himself. The idea that he could be a new person while onstage was exhilarating. From that first play as a munchkin, he listened and observed. He watched the leads rehearse. He dreamed that one day, the lead role would be his.

Every stage became a sanctuary for Kevin, and from then on he would look at empty stages and imagine everyone who might have played there; see the dreams and aspirations of performers and actors who came before him. Joyfully, he would imagine what he could do there. His love for the stage had blossomed, and it would fuel his dreams for the rest of his life.

Chapter 4

Year of Hell

> ***"For the life of me, I cannot believe***
> ***We'd ever die for these sins,***
> ***We were merely freshmen."*** *~Verve Pipe*

If Kevin had been treading through dangerous waters up till now, it was about to get much worse. Living in a new town with no connections and going to an all-boy Catholic school was a recipe for disaster. Ninth grade would strip him of his dignity, his humanity, and his ability to feel anything other than pain and shame. On day one of freshman orientation, his classmates put a liquid laxative into his food at lunch, then proceeded to the restroom to harass and throw things at him while he cowered in the bathroom stall. This was only the beginning.

Every day of that school year brought abuse and pain. His locker was useless as every day his bullies took his keys. They stole or vandalized books, assignments, and personal items alike. They regularly pushed him into fights and confrontations. During showers, he was as likely as not to get a beating. As an adult, Kevin would reflect that his only tattoo was the green dot on his leg from the time a classmate stuck a sharpened pencil in him and broke off the lead tip under his skin.

Kevin's stutter had worsened. Interpersonal communication was nearly impossible. He would rehearse his words in his mind multiple times, and only then would he try to speak them, silently praying for the best.

Near the end of the school year, on *Spirit Day*, the sharks moved in for the kill. It was silly hat day, and Kevin had worn his favorite silly moose hat. As the students sat on the bleachers wearing their silly hats, Kevin once again became a target for the mob, who took his hat and threw it under the bleachers. They pushed him down there, too, as he tried to retrieve it. Then the children in his section began to spit on him. Hot, disgusting saliva and phlegm covered him as he made his way out from under the bleachers.

He knew in that moment he meant nothing to any of them—to anyone. He barely cried walking out of those bleachers. He had finally lost the ability to feel anything at all.

Kevin's classmates didn't seem like real people to him anymore; they all felt like characters in a book that would just vanish when the chapter ended. His empathy was gone along with any shred of humanity and dignity. He felt nothing for others or himself. Life became like one long horror novel of pain.

School administrators were aware that Kevin was a target of abuse. They had been told again and again about the bullying, but they did nothing to protect this child.

On the other hand, they did protect a predator in their midst.

Kevin had taken a job at the school, working directly under a priest who was widely known and respected in the community. Whenever they were alone, his hands found a way to Kevin's body. The grooming was simple in hindsight: First, find a traumatized child and get them alone. Next, point out things they've done wrong, even made-up things like missing money at the end of a shift. Then offer to help them, cover for them, and offer to always be there. Then start groping. Kevin didn't know what to say or do. How could a 14-year-old child have possibly been equipped to handle such a thing?

But when it was time to go to work, Kevin would feel nauseous, have headaches, and body pain. He suddenly started getting sick a lot and could not work anymore. Soon, he was even having problems attending class due to these illnesses. The administration, to cover for their neglect, made sure he passed as long as he would not be going back the next year.

That summer, when the priest found out he would not be coming back, the priest called and spoke to Rosemary on the phone. She said he wanted to take Kevin to a movie and hang out. Kevin felt himself go bleach white. He just said no, went to his room, and trembled until he fell asleep.

Chapter 5

One Bright Spot

"How far that little candle throws his beams!

So shines a good deed in a weary world."

~William Shakespeare, The Merchant of Venice

The stage was still something Kevin loved. In ninth grade, his school partnered with a sister school to produce a series of one-act plays. He knew he had to audition. When another classmate saw that Kevin was signing up, that classmate's expression turned to one of pity and contempt. Seeing that kid's face, such a feeling of self-hatred and despair rose up inside Kevin that he almost scratched his own name off the list and quit before he even tried.

He auditioned and got the male lead for one of the plays. Perfect for him, it was written by Kurt Vonnegut and titled "Who Am I This Time." It follows the life of a man named Harry Nash, known in his small town for his intense shyness. But when Harry takes a part in his local community theater, he embodies a role completely. Whenever he is asked to be in a play, Harry simply asks, "Who am I this time?" This was Kevin, seemingly devoid of self and finding fulfillment in the characters in books. And now, he hoped, under the spotlight. Somehow this came across and he got the role.

The student director, a sweet girl tasked with helping Kevin learn to move about the stage and interact with the female lead, dubbed him *Tin Man*. He was stiff and robotic. The student director accommodated him as best she could. It took them days to teach him how to convincingly put his arm around his lead to start a scene. Kevin had no idea how to have this type of interaction with a girl. He was sweating bullets the entire time.

The day before the play opened, the cast and crew gathered for the dress rehearsal. Most of the cast were dressed for their characters. Unlike most days, Kevin's clothes were clean and pressed, and his hair was neatly combed. One of the girls in the cast wanted to grab ice cream from a little shop down the street and nudged Kevin to go with her. In his mind, that next ninety minutes was about a week and a half of a rom-com movie. They did not kiss, they did not hold hands, they didn't do anything but walk and talk. Well, she talked; Kevin's stuttering made him decide to just listen. But she talked with him. No one had done that, let alone a girl.

It is impossible to ever forget her remarking as they walked back to rehearsal: "You are really cute when you want to be." That compliment was like a flash of lightning going off in the darkest of rooms. For a brief moment, Kevin felt like a person, a moment he has never forgotten.

The play went perfectly, and the confidence from that and the wonderful afternoon the day before buoyed Kevin's spirits. He felt things would be different, now. He cared about how he looked and what he wore. He felt pride he had never felt before. He walked into school on Monday ready to start anew.

In his first-period class, Kevin's bullies started in on him for being in the play. One kid smacked him and another stole everything he could out of his binder. Before the week was out, Kevin would find himself in the gym shower taking another beating.

The feelings of accomplishment and pride drained away, leaving only the realization that the abuse was never going to stop. Kevin had now fallen further than ever before. Any light he had gained was, again, extinguished.

Chapter 6

A List and A Prayer

"Because the greatest love of all

Is happening to me

I found the greatest love of all

Inside of me." *~Whitney Houston*

Kevin was broken and destroyed. His stutter had progressed to the point that he didn't even try to talk anymore, either in public or at home. He had completely lost the ability to communicate. He could not feel real emotion or empathy, that had all been burnt out of him. He could not go on living like this anymore. A new horror had been thrown into the mix: for 10th grade he was going to East Detroit High School, a public high school. Not only would the sophomore class be bigger than any school he had attended, now there would be girls too. He didn't think he had any chance to survive.

So, there he was, 15, wrecked and ready to die. Alone in his bedroom, he couldn't find any joy or reason to keep going. Instead, he ran through every scenario—any conceivable way to end it. To not feel any more pain or loneliness. He knew his mom had pills and taking them with alcohol would make it even more likely to work. There were plenty of knives in the kitchen. One deep cut was all it would take to end it. He thought about doing both just to be sure.

But he also feared that he was such a failure at everything, he would just screw this up as well and leave himself in a vegetative limbo.

The truth was, Kevin was more afraid of living than dying. He knew his dog and parents would be crushed if he died, but he also mistakenly believed they would be better off without someone as useless as him. All he could see was all the pain behind him and the idea that only more pain would follow.

He was also thinking about what lies beyond. The Catholic Church, the Catholic schools, the 'Christians' he had met had all let him down and led him to being hurt and broken. While he believed in God, Kevin wondered if God had ever believed in him. Then a different thought came into Kevin's mind.

What if they were wrong about God?

This was the moment I had the first thought that began to transform me from an observer in Kevin's life into the active conductor in my own life. The thought that would help me to start feeling like my own person. A simple thought that opened a new idea:

What if everyone who had tried to teach me about God was wrong?

What if God didn't inhabit big buildings along with abusive priests? What if God was not about monthly fundraisers and collection plates and kids whose families had connections with the church that got them out of trouble for hurting other kids? What if God was not external? What if God was inside us? I needed to find out what a Higher Power was on a different term. I needed to understand that I could be loved and accepted. That I did not have to be the person who was insulted and bullied. This was not about ignoring the sharks. This was not about hating them. This was about lifting myself to a level above the shark's influence—a level where I could be exactly who I wanted to be. Where the sharks wouldn't matter, and I could rise above and be the person I wanted to see myself as.

If I was going to believe that God was more than what I was taught, it was easy to believe that praying was something different as well. I decided to pray a different kind of prayer. I started to think of a prayer as a call to action: Not a request but a mission statement. A chance to define who and what I wanted to be in clear concrete thoughts and words and actions.

These were a lot of huge thoughts hitting my mind all at once. You will have your own term for spirituality and how it fits into your life. My Christian upbringing shaped my beliefs. This moment solidified them. I cannot say 'Catholic' beliefs because the church had hurt me too badly. But I suddenly saw there could be more for me. I needed to truly decide what I wanted to be if I was going to live, and not just what, but *who*. Who did I want to be from this day forward? Instead of dying, I began to believe I could leave this life I hated behind and start a new one.

I started a list.

I took a pen and paper and wrote down everything I hated about myself. This was an exceptionally long list. My pain had made me withdrawn, bitter, arrogant, and mean. It gave me an arrogant belief that no one else was worth my time. All the hurt had turned me into something very dark and wounded. The more I wrote the more I saw how hurt I was, and how that hurt was lashing out, begging to be healed. It is agonizing to see your pain laid out in black and white in front of you. To look at your flaws and believe they are all your fault—to feel the depression that comes with that belief. The overwhelming sense of dread is like a tidal wave pushing you underwater.

It is particularly hard to examine all this alone. I wish I had understood how to tell others about this pain. Until I saw it written out, I didn't even know how bad it was.

Next, I began another list of all the things I liked about myself. This, sadly, was a noticeably brief list. I liked speaking in front of people. I liked that I could care about my pets. I loved my imagination. I loved the sound of people laughing. There was extraordinarily little I had to pull from. But there was still something. A few good pieces scattered in me. A few seeds that I hoped I could grow a new life from.

Finally, I made a third list: what I wanted to be. This list was complicated. I did not want to be a lot. I mostly just did not want to be in pain. I could not even say I wanted friends as much as I said I just did not want to be hurt. I started writing about qualities TV and novel characters had that I did not. I did not want a superhuman body, I did not want to fly, I just wanted to be accepted. But I didn't even know what being accepted truly meant

I wanted to be nice and kind to the world around me. I did not want revenge or anger. I wanted to spread love and empathy. I wanted to express my humor without being cruel. I wanted to be able to talk. I wanted to feel wanted—to feel love and warmth. I wanted to make friends by being a friend. I just wanted to feel equal to others. To feel worthy of basic human acceptance. While it may not sound like a lot to ask for, it was the difference between life and death.

Looking at this list, for the first time I could see more than the person who existed now and the person who had been. I could see a future for me—a me that I could grow to become and love.

I looked at those lists, and I prayed; I begged God for a chance to be someone different than I had been up to that point—a chance to feel like a person instead of this constant emptiness. This was my mission statement. This is what I would devote myself to and work toward. This was what I prayed for to live. Then, for the first time in forever, I felt calm. Just calm. That night I slept better than I had slept in a long time.

In the morning I folded the list and hid it in my room. That was between God and me. I spent most of that summer alone. Just riding my bike around town and thinking of how I wanted to act. How I wanted to reach out and who I wanted to be. Over and over in my head, I practiced being the person I wanted to be.

But practice soon came to a quick end. Summer was over, and school was in. It was time to go to East Detroit High School and face everything anew.

Chapter 7

Tenth Grade and A New Life

> ***"There's nothing out there you can't do.***
>
> ***Yeah, even Santa Clause believes in you."***
>
> *~The Electric Mayhem*

I tried.

I tried six or seven times to talk to someone, to meet anyone, during orientation, with no luck. I used different approaches to talk to someone, to make a connection and those approaches were failing. I began to panic. Nothing was going to change. I felt like I was going to crash, burn and die.

I took one final chance on the kid in line in front of me getting his books. I saw his name written on his slip.

"Your name's Devin?" I asked. "That's easy to remember. I'm Kevin," I stuttered.

Devin was the opposite of me in so many ways. He looked like a typical punk. He had long hair, Jordache jeans, and an Iron Maiden t-shirt with a flannel. A total 180 from anyone I had been around and exactly who the Catholic schools taught me not to associate with. Perhaps that's why I tried.

Devin and I began to talk. We were both walking home in the same direction. A friendship began that day, and I started to become comfortable and more confident with myself.

Devin introduced me to his friends, and my community began to form. It was not at all the community I expected. My new friends were punks, misfits, and metalheads. My new community was made up of people who accepted me even though I did not dress or act like they did. My house became a second home for Devin and our now-mutual friends, and together we filled it to overflowing with joy and friendship.

Along with the long hair, misfit attitude, and clothes also came the artists. The people who saw the world differently and creatively. My friends could draw, paint, write poetry, and play music. They never criticized each other for it. In fact, every one of them did what they could to elevate each other's artistic side.

I started to really develop as a person. No longer did I feel like someone who was just observing me. I was living my life. I truly felt like I was becoming a real person, not a character in a story. I was starting to become *me*.

My mom became everyone's mom. She was always there with an ear, a hug, and a sassy retort. There were oxymorons to her speaking pattern. She would love and insult you all in the same sentence, like "I love you, you son of bitch," and "Glad you came over, now get out of here." But it was always done with love. We all understood her words for the love they came wrapped in.

My dad became something even more to us. My friend Bill gave him the nickname *Papa Chuck*. Whenever Papa Chuck was home, so many of my friends were waiting to talk to him. He answered their questions honestly and without judgment. He listened when someone had a problem and was always there to lend support, advice, and honesty. Sometimes very brutal honesty, starting with such classic phrases as, "Are you really that stupid?" or, "Pretend I'm smiling because I don't have time to answer nicely." But my friends knew he cared about them and took it in stride and gratitude.

I also auditioned for the fall play and was cast in a small speaking role. This was huge for me. The drama teacher, Mrs. Pietryck, would become a huge influence in my life. She saw in me a talent and a desire to put it to work. Throughout high school, she would be an incredible guide for me. She was patient with me when I screwed up and hard on me when I needed a push—everything a great teacher should be.

The cast expanded my community of friends and feeling of belonging. This would lead to my first kiss! I remember walking her home in the opposite direction of my house and talking the entire way with her. I remember that first taste of her lipstick and feeling like I could do anything.

While that kiss was exciting and exhilarating, it was nothing compared to the tapping lesson.

Between Devin and the play, my friends allowed me space to speak even with my stutter. I began to tap as a metronome for my words. Whether I was tapping the stage, my leg, or a pencil on a table, the steady beat allowed me to sound out each syllable. I couldn't easily say, "do you understand?" but I could tap out the syllables *do-you-un-der-stand*. I felt like a weirdo, but I also felt confident because these people gave me room and permission to do what I needed to communicate. Within six months most of my stutter had cleared. I had a voice again—a real voice—and friends to share it with.

For the first time in my life, I really felt included and a part of something. I could feel myself growing. A few people who knew me before I came to East Detroit High School went out of their way to tell me how much happier and content I seemed. No one bullied me. It would not have mattered if they'd tried. I had a community that offered me support no bully could take away. I enjoyed that year so much I was almost sorry for the school year to end.

I'm grateful it did though because I had an amazing summer ahead of me.

Chapter 8

Camp Counseling

> ***"We are the C.I.T.'s***
>
> ***So, pity us.***
>
> ***The kids are brats***
>
> ***The food is hideous!"*** *~Meatballs*

That summer I had a job waiting for me working on a Scout Ranch. I had applied for the job before the school year even started. I was hoping to work on the horse ranch side, but it turned out another department wanted me as well, and as they pointed out, I'd do a lot less shoveling of horse manure on the skill-building side. My position at the camp would be to help young scouts just beginning their scouting adventure.

It was odd to feel no anxiety about leaving my friends for the summer, as I knew they would be there when I got back. Normally I would be afraid that people would walk out of my life if I was not available. I wasn't afraid of my friends turning on me or talking behind my back. It was easy to check in with my friends while at camp, since most of them were hanging at my house with Mom and Dad.

The scout camp was wonderful and continued to build me up. I had learned a lot in scouting over the years, and my skills were appreciated. I made a great community, even establishing a dear friendship with the camp chaplain, who would be a valued presence in my life for many years to come. He listened as I told him my story of abuse. He was kind and compassionate. His ability to listen and answer with love and empathy really gave my resentment of the church a little bit of relief.

I got to work alongside scouts from all different backgrounds, including an 18-year-old exchange scout from England named Claire. She was an amazing person who at 18 decided to live a summer in a whole different country. We worked together and became friends. I learned a lot about travel from her, and she created a desire in me to experience diverse cultures. I also learned a lot from her about the value of listening.

There were two staff cabins. Mine was more closely related to the misfits of the swamp from M*A*S*H* than orderly scouts. We had to be at breakfast every morning at 8 a.m. in full uniform. Inevitably at about 7:45 every morning someone would scream: "The alarm didn't go off" and we would all run to breakfast getting dressed on the way. There was even the joy of a shaving cream fight in the cabin.

Before, I had run from anything resembling a shaving cream fight. There was no sense of fun for me in things like that, only the dread and fear of more sharks coming to attack. But here, it was friends having fun and laughing with each other. I was getting ready for a dinner, and I was nervous about speaking to a group. One of the guys said it would be worse to speak while covered in shaving cream and began to hose me down white foam. We were both laughing hysterically. Once he'd emptied the can, he loaned me his shirt, embroidered with his higher rank insignia, so I would be ready. Instead of feeling attacked and victimized, I felt accepted. I thought my heart could not be any fuller than that moment.

Yet one moment was even better: As the clock ticked midnight turning June 21 into June 22 it was now my sixteenth birthday. An alarm went off and everyone in my cabin sang "Happy Birthday" to me. I had to choke back the tears. I will never know how to say thank you enough.

No sharks circled, hoping to smell blood. I had found more of my school of fish to swim with.

One year before, I had been alone, hurt, and ready to die. Now I had a community celebrating me.

Chapter 9

Community

Today I don't need a replacement

I'll tell them what the smile on my face meant

My heart going "Boom-boom-boom,"

"Hey," I said. "You can keep my things,

They've come to take me home." *~Peter Gabriel*

It would take me many years to put everything that happened in my tenth-grade year into focus. To really look back and understand what had changed. In hindsight, I understand that the key difference is community.

There were still sharks—people who can only build themselves up by tearing others down. Those people just didn't matter to me anymore. While in nature a shark will attack a school of fish, in human life, it's different. It's difficult for someone to emotionally bully you when you're part of a supportive community—when you no longer care what the sharks think because you're surrounded by fish who value the same things you do. A shark cannot attack or take away my self-esteem when their point of view means nothing to me. Why would I care what some people thought of what I wore or what I did when I had friends who supported me no matter what? It is hard to be emotionally bullied when you have a community you feel a part of. A community that makes you feel emotionally strong. It's also a lot harder for a bully to physically attack you when you're hanging out with a group of friends.

A group of fish is known as a *school*. That is what I believe a community should be: a school guiding you and teaching you. Like a proper school, your community should listen to your ideas as you listen to theirs. You should be able to learn from the differences in others while feeling comfortable in your own. The community should consistently build you up to be your best self as you do the same for each of your fellow community members.

It can be hard to find a community when you have felt isolated for so long. It is easy to fear a community you do not understand. It is even harder to find the right community. The right community helps you build your strengths and your sense of self. The right community will not sacrifice you for their own pleasure.

Some people think the fact that I found the outcasts as my community is a potential negative. They were the burnouts; some would even be dropouts. But it was never negative. I never felt peer pressure. Being raised by Chuck, I never saw a positive side to drinking or drugs. Now that I'd found my *home* in this circle of friends, the idea of escaping was the last thing on my mind. I wanted to embrace every moment. I did not smoke, drink, or do drugs, and my friends didn't care. It meant more for them. Hell, they would eventually love having a designated driver always available. They saw the world differently than I did, yet they never belittled me for my point of view. They encouraged my dreams. So many people were confused to see two rows of leather jackets and heavy metal t-shirts at a high school play, but my school of fish was there to support me just as I was there to support and encourage them.

I never felt comfortable in the *popular* cliques. That's on me. I always felt less than, not because of the *popular kids*, but because of me. I was friendly with most everyone, including jocks, preps, geeks, and everyone in between. I just never felt at ease in the *in-groups*—I always felt like an imposter. It's something I still battle against. We all have those voices of insecurity in our head—the ones that tell you you're not welcome. It is hard to ignore that voice and take the chance. Sometimes that voice might be correct. In my own life, I have found that voice is often wrong and there are so many people waiting to welcome you into a new setting.

I learned having a community that wanted me to be my best helped me grow beyond who I was. They wanted me to grow into the best version of me. I had a long way to go, but one step at a time, I was getting there.

Chapter 10

High School Opens Its Heart

"Seize upon that moment long ago

One breath away and there you will be

So young and carefree

Again, you will see

That place in time... so gold." *~Stevie Wonder*

Junior year really allowed me to branch out. I was taking drama and speaking classes, both of which I excelled at. My ability to speak in public had grown by leaps and bounds. Even better, though, was that these skills meant that my interpersonal communication, talking to individuals was finally something that I could do. I was overjoyed to be able to carry on conversations. I was working as a pizza flipper and thanks to my friends, I was having a fun time.

That year I had a dream come true: I got the lead in the spring play. This was not just any play: this was *The Outsiders*, one of my favorite books and movies of all time. I would play Ponyboy, the main character! I fought hard for that role. I did everything I could to not just make the audition perfect, but to make it clear how much I wanted it and how hard I would work for it. Ironically, my main competition for the role came from the same kid who almost stopped me from auditioning in ninth grade. Thankfully, Mrs.

Pietryck thought I was the best for the role. I was ready to be the lead.

And my competitor? During the production, he became one of my biggest cheerleaders and the first to congratulate me on getting the role.

This was the first time I felt what it meant to have a cast not only count on me to perform the role but believe in me and my ability to do it. Of course, there were the usual practical jokes, but it was all in fun and never meant to hurt me. At one point in the show, my character got dunked in a fountain. There was not one performance where someone didn't fill it with ice water. During rehearsals, costumes would disappear mid-change. Any script left on the stage to help an actor stay on track would inevitably be replaced with something completely inappropriate. With all the joking, I knew I could trust my fellow cast members to do their best as well.

I did take one of the hardest slaps of my life in that show, though it wasn't intentional. My character's big brother was played by the head of the football team. While we practiced blocking the scene where he smacks me many times, on opening night it looked perfect. That was because the adrenaline got to him, and he legitimately smacked me across the stage. I have never seen an audience so convinced a moment was real—nor have I seen anyone more apologetic after.

There was one night of that production when no jokes were played at all. In fact, I have never seen a high school group work so hard as the night a college scout came to watch me. Everyone did their best to make sure I shined, and I really did. The college scout was really pleased, and we would talk over the next two years about attending their college and available scholarships.

That play sticks in my memory for all the punks and misfits, my friends, filling the auditorium as well. Those friends, my fish, helped me build the confidence to feel like a real person. They made me believe that I could be proud of myself. That I was a valued member of the community. The more I found honesty and community, the more I could grow. The more I could contribute and add to the community. I was beginning to understand self-confidence—to learn what it meant to believe in myself and others. It would take a long time for me to really understand how many people were there for me and cared for me. I had yet to truly understand the idea of object permanence when it came to friendships. The idea that even when out of sight, the people who cared about you would be there. But I was starting to figure it out.

A bigger community was about to open the world of my dreams.

Chapter 11

Jokers All Around

"Clowns to the left of me,

Jokers to the right." *~Steelers Wheel*

I became a professional performer the day before my 17th birthday. A simple job opportunity would launch my entire career, and I didn't even know it.

I was always looking for opportunities to get paid to be on stage. I'd answered an audition for a party company called Jokers R Wild run by David Anthony. His company supplied entertainment for private parties, and he needed more people as costume characters for children's birthday parties.

I showed up to the office on a Saturday morning, as agreed, to shadow David as he performed. By office, I mean the basement of David's mom's house. David had forgotten I was coming. He had also forgotten a costume for the next party. He came back to the office to find me waiting, and my life changed.

I had no idea what I was getting into.

First, you may know someone with as much outgoing charisma as David, but I guarantee you do not know anyone with more. Perpetually upbeat, his boundless energy made him the center of attention. He had the unrelenting smile of a kid on Christmas that lit up every room he walked into. He combined the body of a Chippendale dancer, the outgoing energy of a kid's performer, and the compassion to want to see everyone around him do great.

I will never forget that first day. I watched David do four shows and helped him steal helium balloons from a senior center because he forgot to bring his own. He performed each show as a character like a Purple Dinosaur, a Karate Turtle, or a magical jester (for trademark reasons they definitely didn't have *Barney*, *Ninja Turtles*, or a *Genie*). Driving between shows, he explained the business while I asked a ton of questions. Then fate stepped in, and on the way to his last booking of that day, the office called. One of the other performers' cars broke down and they could not make their last show.

"I can do it!"

"You can?" asked David.

I responded with the words that have defined every moment of my career from that second to this one:

"No, but I can fake it for an hour."

Next thing I knew, I was in a *Karate Turtle* (red one!) for the next hour until someone at the office could pick me up). I played every game I knew, told every story I had, did everything I remembered David doing, and still had about 40 more minutes to fill. I just played with the kids till my ride showed up.

I played—performed—for an hour and got $40 for it! That's more than I made in a week at the pizza place. I had become a professional entertainer.

Everyone at Jokers was patient with this 17-year-old kid. I did shows on my own and followed other performers on their shows to learn more. The company needed more clowns, and I wanted more shows, so I learned clowning, which would teach me balloon-twisting and a little bit of magic. The magic took off and became a big passion of mine. I pushed myself to get better at performing magic daily. Within a year I became one of their top magicians.

I had known for some time that I wanted to do something on stage as a career. Now here was a chance to do it—to build my own show, my own self, into something people wanted to see. I didn't understand everything that would come with it, but my career had truly begun.

I learned so much at Jokers R Wild. This was my first introduction to entertaining people in one of the most challenging environments: their own homes. I was the stranger in the room and had to make friends out of everyone fast. I had to keep the kids entertained and live up to the parents' expectations. All while being a very green performer with a lot yet to learn. But learn I did.

I learned to keep audience attention on me and to fill a room with my show. I learned to make an effect simple to understand to get the biggest response. I learned to listen to kids' answers when I asked questions. I started learning how to turn an audience into friends.

I also started learning about worlds far beyond the one I grew up in. I performed in houses of the extraordinarily rich and houses of the extremely poor. The Detroit area was a melting pot of so many cultures that I got to experience parties and food I would never have otherwise seen. But one thing always stayed the same: if I treated my audience and clients with respect, more times than not they did the same for me.

I also began to learn a little bit about the business side of things. David needed help filing three years of contracts, and I agreed to do it. Anything beat flipping pizzas. One of the remarkable things Jokers R Wild would do is follow up comments with the clients. I got to read the notes on everyone's shows, including mine. A lot of the reviews were fantastic; some were heartbreaking. I quickly realized if one person had a negative comment, I could usually blow it off. If three or more people had the same comment, I had something to work on.

These reviews helped me to continue crafting who I was when I performed. People loved the high energy I brought, but not the fact that I talked too fast to understand. They loved how I spent time with everyone at the show, but not when I would show up looking rushed because I was running late. These first lessons helped to start the process of forging the performer I would one day become.

I once asked David why he was not famous. He told me: "Never become comfortable. Comfort kills drive."

I took that to heart. I always tried to push myself out of my comfort zone and to grow as a performer. Eventually, as people do, I outgrew that company. I wish I'd had the wisdom to leave properly. I did not. I would leave the company after great years of shows with a temper tantrum because I did not know how to move forward respectfully.

Thanks to David's heart, I never burned my bridge with him. I'm lucky he always stayed a friend, a guide, and a mentor.

Chapter 12

Senior Year

> ***"I sing the body electric***
>
> ***I celebrate the me yet come***
>
> ***I toast to my own reunion***
>
> ***When I become one with the sun."*** *~Fame*

My senior year did a lot to begin to grow my future. I found out office co-op was a thing. I could spend half the school day working and getting paid, which was awesome. But first I had to defeat my arch nemesis at the time: my guidance counselor.

This guy missed every honor roll I was on, any award I received, and was just generally useless to my high school career. He told me I wouldn't be allowed to take the office co-op as I needed to get a swimming credit.

I'd missed gym during my sophomore year due to ankle surgery, and now that—with the help of the person who had never helped guide me at all—was going to stop me from doing something that would grow my life in ways I could never imagine.

"Sorry Kevin, you need a swimming credit," he said.

"I don't," I replied. "I'll have my doctor give you a note about why I can't take swimming, then I'll take the co-op."

“Life doesn’t work that way,” he countered.

“I’ll be back in thirty minutes,” I told him as I stormed out.

My doctor listened to about thirty seconds of my story before giving me the note of medical exemption. Handing that note to my guidance counselor with a smug look on my face was fun.

My counselor reacted with a shrug and said, “Ok, you can’t take swimming. You can take the office co-op. Is there anything else I can do?”

“Just stay out of my way,” was all I said.

I know how this makes me sound: I was being petulant and petty. I still had a lot of distrust for adults and authority. For most of my life, those people who were supposed to keep me safe had fed me to the sharks. It took me a long time to trust the people who were there to help. Honestly, when I think about what this co-op would mean for my future, I shudder to think of what might have happened had I lost it.

My co-op job was working for Al Bara, curriculum coordinator for the Junior High School. He really had no idea how to use me, so mostly I helped the office assistants.

About two months into my job Al found out I was doing magic. He had an idea for me and told me about this new program called D.A.R.E, the new anti-drug program for schools. His idea was for me to put together a few magic tricks that would align with the program’s principles and present them at the D.A.R.E. assemblies along with participating D.A.R.E. Officers. These shows became a hit. Al started to get me booked doing D.A.R.E. style school assemblies for the elementary schools in town. Working for one school led to working for two more and so on. Then Al had an even better idea—he was going to fire me!

This would be the best firing of all time. He knew my skills could be better used in a different department. Instead of working for him, he got me moved to the D.A.R.E. office, which was also the Community Networking Center for the city of East Detroit (now Eastpointe).

At the Networking Center, I worked alongside the police department, city hall, and the chamber of commerce. This led to shows for the city, the chamber of commerce, and local businesses. Al opened my world by giving me an opportunity and then providing guidance to help me get the most out of it. I like to think I've made the most of opportunities when they present themselves, but here was someone so early on showing how I could also begin to build my own career.

My work with D.A.R.E. led to winning my city's *Youth of the Year Award*. I found out afterward that Al, the police department, the D.A.R.E. officers, and multiple elementary principals had nominated me. By the time the city councilmen tried to nominate me, they were told it was already a done deal. The little nerdy kid who had once had no friends was now receiving an award for outstanding service to his city.

It did come with a bit of an attitude problem—I no longer had a fear of calling out the adults who I felt wronged me.

At the luncheon for the award would be my guidance counselor and a couple of other administrators who had been only obstacles when I needed support. I resented them. I was going to have a microphone and the ability to say anything I wanted. My speech was going to open with the line:

“This award goes to my guidance counselor, and senior advisor, without whose help I still earned this award.” The speech would go downhill from there.

I still held strong resentments.

My friends knew that my speech was going to involve calling administrators out, and somehow Mrs. Pietryck found out, as well. I’m guessing one of my wiser friends tipped her off.

“I heard about the opening to your speech.” Said Mrs. P, pulling me aside before class. “You have earned the right to say anything you’d like to say and to whoever you want to say it about. Out of kindness for me, would you please open with something kinder.”

“For you,” I replied with heartfelt respect for all she had done, “consider it changed.”

She knew if I said what I wanted to, it wouldn’t make me look like the best version of me, and I couldn’t say no to her. She had built me up too much to let her down by being petty, so I skipped that speech.

She also helped me skip school, so it was more than fair.

Second City was opening in Detroit, and I wanted to audition during school hours. All Mrs. P asked was if I thought I would be cast. I didn’t think I would, but I wanted to learn from the audition process. She agreed I would learn a lot, and off I went. I had no idea what improv really was, and no idea how to prepare. I totally failed the audition but won something bigger: I asked the judges if I could stay and watch the other auditions. I wanted to learn more about what judges were looking for and what the other auditioners were doing. At first, they seemed confused, but when they realized I was sincere, they agreed to let me stay. In between auditions, they even answered a lot of questions that would help me grow. They gave me pointers about improv guidelines and ideas about where to learn more. Mostly, they just gave me time and attention.

I also got to cut school on a Friday to be part of a weekend-long audition workshop being taught by a Chicago casting agent. After the first half day, I knew I was out of my league. When I asked the administrator how I had even gotten into this limited-space event, I got a great answer.

"With the tenacity that you called us with and showed at the audition we knew it would be easier for us to let you in than keep you out," the director told me. That enthusiastic tenacity would stay with me my entire career.

The two plays we did my senior year were a huge education. I got to write my own part as the narrator for *Sleeping Beauty*. Mrs. P wanted me to use the skills I'd learned doing kids' shows to open and close each act. It was a lot of fun and I got to explore the idea of just being me. Much more challenging was our production of *Fame*. Lacking singing and dancing skills, there wasn't a significant role in the show for me. But one thing I had yet to do was really work on the other side of a production. Mrs. P selected me to be the student director. Auditioning, casting, designing, and rehearsing were now on my shoulders. I learned a lot about working with people and personalities. I also learned that I hated that part of production. While I enjoy writing and performing, I will gladly leave the technical side of things to those who are far better at it than I am.

Graduation was bittersweet, but I was excited about all the opportunities in front of me. Almost attached to my graduation was something else I was extremely proud of: earning my Eagle Scout Award. Less than 1 in 200 scouts earn this coveted award. After changing towns, I had changed scout troops a couple of times until I found one that I liked—one that helped me grow and earn that award. My parents were proud, and so was I. The idea of earning the Eagle Award was about personal achievement. It was about going out and achieving something on my own. Graduating High School was easy. All I had to do was show up to graduate. Earning that Eagle is not hard, but you have to put in the work to do it. No one else could do it for me. It made me part of another group of fish that would build me up. Scouting helped teach me independence, and with the summer camp job, it taught me how to be part of a community.

It was a great Eagle ceremony. The mayor, city council, and state representatives all came out. Many teachers and family friends were there. Once again, what I love about my memory of that day is not just the local dignitaries who show up to something like that, it was all the leather jackets of my friends who showed up once again to support me. My friends were proud of me. No one made fun of me for being in scouts. They were thrilled by my accomplishment.

The kid who only three years ago had no one now had friends, dreams, and growing talents. I had a community that would be there with me. I was leaving high school, but not leaving my school of fish. I'd had so many positive experiences. My career as a performer had begun. All because I chose to live and reach out to people. Because I was willing to be a friend and receive friendship; because I was willing to listen and learn.

After graduation, I re-read the lists I'd made the day I wanted to die. I looked at everything I had become compared to the person I was when I wrote them. I felt like a phoenix risen from the ashes. I could cry tears of joy over the fact that I had achieved everything I had wanted to become. I could thank God my prayer had been answered. I wish I had saved the list, but instead, at that moment, I chose to burn it. It was an offering to God and myself. A way of letting go of the past. I could give thanks for every day I had lived from that moment.

I was ready to start my path to adulthood.

Chapter 13

Don and Bill

"Whenever this world is cruel to me

I got you to help me forgive

Ooh, you make me live." *~Queen*

None of us go through it alone. There are people who become part of our journey along the way. If you can count on even one hand the people who are there for you, you are an incredibly lucky person. Throughout my life, I've been beyond fortunate for great people who have come into and out of my life. Even more fortunate for all the people who have stayed in my life through good and bad. Two of them have been there through thick and thin since high school.

I met Don through Devin, and we quickly became brothers. We were there for each other no matter the situation. Girlfriend troubles bonded us even more. We were both in negative relationships that we didn't know how to handle. We were able to help each other to figure out how to move on. From that moment on, he and I have always been there no matter what.

Don and I did everything together. We laughed about the same movies and comics. We always found a way to lighten up a situation and not let things rest too heavy on the other's shoulders. As I rose in my career, it was like I had to be two people, and Don became that second person. He would help me set up gigs and then assist in the shows as a stagehand. He could always find a way to make things better. Most importantly, he would put me out when I lit myself on fire (Literally. More than once).

Don and I would take road trips and work every nightclub we could find. We ended up backstage at major events meeting awesome people. We even headlined *Lollapalooza's* 3rd stage in Detroit and also for *H.O.R.D.E. Fest*. He was excited when we did charity work with Power Play Productions, the charity founded by Gordie and Colleen Howe (Mr. and Mrs. Hockey™). He got to meet some of hockey's greats. Of all the gigs we did together, those were his favorites.

Through every hard gig, mishap, and fire issue, he helped push me up when I didn't think I could do it. He was a rock when I was unsteady and a grounding presence when my head was too far in the clouds. He is a brother and always will be.

Don's career path took him into the medical field. Sometimes he credits all the crazy shows we did for his ability to stay sane as an EMT and surgical tech.

The only time I have ever been angry with him was when we were nineteen. I found out his girlfriend was pregnant, and he'd kept it a secret from me. He was afraid it would push me away because it had pushed others away. It didn't and it couldn't. I made sure he knew I would be there with him every step of the way. I was excited to join him on the journey. I have loved his daughter, my niece, Kendra, from the second she was born. I am so proud of her as a person, and I am beyond proud of Don's skill as a dad.

Of the two of us, Don was always far more traditional and grounded. His level-headedness kept me saner than anyone else could have. I am so thankful to have him as a brother in my life.

On the other side of that coin is my friendship with Bill.

Bill came to live with me and my parents during my senior year of high school. We had mutual friends and were close. Bill's story is complicated, but it involves him being emancipated from his family at an early age. At the time he had long, curly blonde hair and wore a leather trench coat with chains. Picture an angry metal-head version of Michael Bolton and you can imagine Bill at that age. He was troubled, yet he pushed himself and got himself through high school and college. He only lived with my family for a brief time, but we became great friends who would inspire each other.

The moment that really made me realize the strength of our bond was the day a mutual friend of ours decided I needed to be set straight. The mutual friend took me out for a long lunch and told me everything I was doing wrong. How my dreams were just that: dreams. A hobby. How I needed to focus on a real career and get on the real-life path as soon as possible or else. This was shocking to me, as I thought this person supported my dreams. Bill knew this conversation was going to happen and called me after I got home.

"Do you agree with what he said?" Bill asked.

"No, I don't think I do," was my response. "I think I'm doing what I should be."

"Good," said Bill. "Do not let anyone who has given up on a dream or goal tell you to give up on yours."

More important words were never spoken. Any time I got down on my dreams, Bill found a way to give me hope. When I got lazy, he found a way to challenge or motivate me. I did the same for him. There was not any situation he or I could face where the other would not be there to offer guidance, an idea, or a helping hand. We would always be there to elevate each other. As friends do, Bill and I lost touch for a couple of years. As soon as we got back in touch it was like no time had passed at all and we were right back to building each other up.

Bill and Don even ended up as roommates at one point, which made it even easier for the three of us to do everything together. It was often said that Don, Bill, and I shared a brain. If one of us could not think straight one day, it was "his day without the brain." The three of us always stood together.

There's a Hagar the Horrible comic with three Vikings trying to take a castle. Hagar says (to paraphrase): "The walls are too high; we cannot climb it. The moat is too wide; we cannot swim it."

Lucky Eddie replies, "Too bad there isn't one more of us, we could surround it." Well, the three of us could surround anything!

Chapter 14

Lili's 21

> ***"Cause I've got friends in low places***
> ***Where the whiskey drowns and the***
> ***beer chases my blues away."*** *~Garth Brooks*

At 19, I was working at private parties and small company events, but knew my act was like a lot of others. Detroit is a blue-collar town, and that extended to entertainment. I was told there was a way I was supposed to perform to get the gig. I was told I had to be like other performers to get the job. I didn't want to be like the other performers. I wanted to do something unique and make people laugh.

I needed to find a place to open myself up to performing in ways I wanted to perform. I wanted to develop a show where audiences wanted to see me, not a trick.

Thankfully, a friend dragged me to where I needed to go: Lili's 21 in Hamtramck, MI. Lili's 21 was the biggest little punk club in Michigan. It was every bar in every Tom Waits song. It was dark, seedy, and just what I needed to grow. It would barely hold 150 people packed, but everyone had played there back in the day: Iggy Pop, the New York Dolls, even the Goo Goo Dolls. When the band *Sponge* had a number one song on the radio they came and did a

Lili's 21 show out of gratitude for all the support Lili's had given them.

At some point, someone had convinced Lili's management to do a poetry open mic night on Mondays. My friend Darius wanted to attend and brought me along with him. It was a night that would grow my life and community more than I could have imagined.

To be honest, I had no idea why I was going to a poetry open mic. I had no idea what Lili's 21 was. Thankfully, none of that mattered. The first thing that did matter was that the poets were excited a non-poet had shown up. Performing magic and comedy was viewed as a breath of fresh air and something different to break up the night. Best of all was the bartender, Mike, who had been a magician as a kid and was still a fan. I ended up spending far more time with Mike than with the poets.

Every week I would show up and talk to Mike and try some new things on stage. I got to know the regulars there, affectionately referred to as the Group W bench (a reference from the song *Alice's Restaurant* by Arlo Guthrie, *Group W* being unfit for military duty due to criminal records). Mike and the regulars really helped me see performing in a new light. They wanted me to do well, but they were easily bored by bullshit. They'd throw bottles at you if they liked you! If I wanted to keep their attention, I had to give them a premise and a direct result. Long-winded stories with no payoff were an invitation for heckling. Sharp, to-the-point routines earned applause and rapt attention.

Mike's brother Art (former frontman for *The Mutants*) was the booker for Lili's 21, and Mike convinced Art to try something different between bands on weekend nights, especially when there was a novelty band playing. Art booked me to emcee between bands and gave me the name *Kevin the Uncanny*. It caught on.

Soon bands would request me to open for them in other venues. A great band, *The Immortal Winos of Soul* even took me on road gigs with them. I was performing for drunk adult crowds, but slowly I was learning to keep their attention—what they liked and what they ignored. I was learning that it wasn't as much about the trick as it was about the performer. I was learning how to be me.

I had many great nights at Lili's 21. That little club adopted me and helped me grow up in a lot of ways. Again, my school of fish had grown. In hindsight, it's easy to see how they made sure I was around for good times and kept me away from bad influences, but at the time I had no idea. I didn't realize anything bad ever happened to anyone there. I never saw drugs there because I was not allowed to see them. I was never put into a situation with anyone doing anything harmful because everyone knew to keep that away from *the kid*.

The folks at Lili's really did create a nurturing environment for me, letting me hang out and drink soda when I needed to get away from the rest of the world. They would listen to me and offer me advice. There was a lot of wisdom on a barstool for a 19-year-old kid who was willing to listen. There was horrible advice, as well.

Thankfully, the times I didn't have the wisdom to figure out which was which, Mike would point me in the right direction.

Chapter 15

My First Mental Break Down

> ***"Well, it seems to me that you***
> ***Have seen too much in too few years***
> ***And though you've tried you just***
> ***Can't hide your eyes are edged with tears."*** *~The Rolling Stones*

You may notice a couple of running themes through this book: one is finding your community, and another is seeking help when you need it.

It's not always easy to know when you need to ask for help. We all assume our brains work like everyone else's. We don't always notice when our brains are behaving differently from others, or impacting us negatively, because this is the only brain we've ever had. As I grew up, there were a lot of signs that I suffered from ADHD and depression. Unfortunately, the adults around me didn't recognize or understand them. Schools never discovered my issues because I was clever enough to hide them. I'd turn in zero homework, but I could hyper-focus and pass exams. My parents never had the chance to notice, as my brother's problems were so extreme that my mental health looked fine by comparison. I did not know how to admit I was hurting.

I was nineteen and trying to manage my career. That meant I was my own business and my own paycheck. I had to work as much as I could during busy times and try to budget myself to get through the lean times. I worked gigs on weekends and holidays all the time, missing out on weekend trips with friends.

On top of the usual stresses of managing my own business, I had my own insecurities running through my head. I feared I would never earn enough to make a living. Anytime I wasn't actively doing a show, I felt like I was failing everyone who believed in me. Nothing I did felt good enough. I was in a relationship that was not building me up. I was running 100 miles per hour and didn't feel like I was getting anywhere.

I was getting *somewhere* though; I was getting closer to a breakdown.

This breakdown resulted from a combination of factors. The main factor was that my brain chemicals were out of balance. I needed medication I didn't know existed. My depression made my career look impossible. It made me believe I was a failure—like I didn't know how to grow my life or achieve anything. That frustration led to self-anger. Anger can be like rocket fuel for your motivation. It can push you and move you forward. Unfortunately, as a mentor would tell me, anger is like having rocket fuel in a ship with no guidance system. My brain snapped.

I remember yelling at a friend, throwing away my car keys, and walking into the night muttering to myself. I remember walking down the middle of streets just totally numb. My friend would eventually find me and get me into their car. They bought me a soda and NyQuil, took me home, and told my parents. I went to Community Mental Health the next day.

I met a great doctor who misread *magician* as *musician* on my intake form and was shocked I was not covered in tattoos. I was his first magician. He started me on antidepressants, which came with a lot of side effects I didn't like. In the short term, the medication helped me immensely. In the long term, it made everything gray and numb. Antidepressant medications have come a long way since then and are so much more helpful to many more people. At the time I knew I needed to improve, and I was incredibly lucky to find a doctor and a treatment that worked for me.

Talking to a doctor regularly helped me get the medication I needed and learn coping skills. I also learned there were things I could do to help get me off the medication. My friends jumped on those with me. They would drag me if I didn't want to walk—this is not a metaphor. They would pick me up out of bed and force me to exercise. They pushed me to talk openly and honestly about how I was feeling—they wanted to talk about what was going on in my mind. When they did not have genuine advice to help me deal with frustration, they helped me find someone who did.

In the meantime, my community helped me to grow beyond and achieve. Unfortunately, the root of my problem was still there. It would be years before I confronted that.

Chapter 16

Hypnosis

> ***"That's why it seems like a dream***
>
> ***Got me hypnotized***
>
> ***And I know that's right."*** *~Fleetwood Mac*

What would you do differently if you knew one moment would change your life? I did not know that day walking into the Michigan Holistic Health Center that I would learn the skill that would take me all over the world and make me a Vegas headliner. All I knew was that I wanted to learn something new.

By this point, I had been making my living doing magic and fire-eating. I had seen hypnotists perform at events, but it didn't seem like something I could ever do. Nothing about it seemed accessible, and neither did the hypnotists I met. Most of them seemed more interested in actively discouraging people from learning.

But a few were kind enough to talk to me about it, and those conversations sparked an interest. This was 1995. The internet was barely a thing, and the available books on hypnosis were not particularly helpful. I needed training.

I learned how to eat fire from watching a video. This was not the safest way to learn. I injured myself a few times. Thankfully, most of the time Don was there with a fire extinguisher to put me out. I knew hypnosis involved other people, so I wanted to learn hypnosis in a much more professional manner. After a lengthy search, I finally found someone who taught Clinical Hypnotherapy in the Detroit area. The problem was that he had no interest in teaching a stage performer, let alone a 20-year-old kid. The course was designed for clinical workers.

What I said next, I do not recommend, but I was young and didn't see another choice. I told him:

"I've read a few books on hypnosis. I could either go out and screw some people up, or you can teach me how to do it correctly and I'll make it a positive experience for everyone who sees it."

Maybe he saw my point, maybe he respected my brash attitude, maybe he just wanted the tuition money, but he gave in and welcomed me into the class. It was a 3-month course, all day Saturdays and Sundays with homework throughout the week. At the end of three months, I would get my certification as a Hypnotherapist. I knew I didn't want to do therapy, but I believed this would teach me to do hypnosis correctly and safely.

The course was $1500. My grandmother had a small college account for her grandkids, and this would be my *college*. It made her nervous to think that my education would be in hypnosis, but she believed in me. I enrolled.

The class sucked. The teacher repeated himself often and rambled even more. In hindsight, I don't know whether he did not know how to teach hypnosis or if he just did not have the right knowledge to share. Also, at that time there were not a lot of other resources to reach out and learn from.

I absorbed every piece of knowledge I could find on hypnosis. I also knew the only way I would truly grow was to get experience.

The class at least taught me how to use hypnosis safely, so I started doing shows. Small shows, high school schools, coffee shops, anywhere that would give me a chance. The shows felt good and inch-by-inch improved. When they saw me making money, many magicians I knew who had laughed at me for taking the course enrolled in one as well. Others belittled me, claiming hypnosis was too simple, yet none of them could do it.

It would be a few years before the hypnosis show would really take off. I wanted to write something that was different and more positive than what I was seeing out there. I wanted it to be uplifting, not humiliating. I also needed to learn from other performers and professionals the things the teacher could not teach me, like how to work with crowds, how to choose an audience participant (and who not to choose), and how to get the best out of everyone who volunteered for the show. It would take me years, but I did learn.

I learned that most of it came from empathy.

If the years of abuse taught me anything they taught me how to feel or sympathize with what others are going through. Empathy taught me to put myself in other people's shoes. That was one of the big moments that would grow my show—the moment I learned to look at everyone on my stage as members of my school of fish, seeing them as people and wanting the best for them. Most hypnotists at that time I saw as sharks. They wanted to show their power by forcing someone to humiliate themselves for a laugh. I refused to do it that way. I wanted my school of fish to be stars and treated them as such.

I think a lot of hypnosis shows have evolved and most hypnotists who treat their volunteers well do great. The world is weeding out more people who try to bully or embarrass people for fun. But misconceptions remain about hypnosis shows and hypnosis itself.

People think hypnosis is something done to you or forced upon you. Nothing could be further from the truth. Everything affects our minds and our views constantly. The act of wanting to be hypnotized allows you to be hypnotized. The desire to engage with a hypnotist gives your brain the desire to enter that state.

There are videos all over the internet that show what looks like people being forced into hypnosis. There are also videos all over with people flying and turning into werewolves. Some people need to look at hypnosis as a way to project their own personal power. Hypnotists who practice this way rarely have careers. The hypnotists who succeed the most are those who truly want to share hypnosis with others, whether in a clinical or a stage setting. Hypnotists who work with people do much better than those trying to inflict themselves upon others. Most hypnosis is rapport. The more comfortable you feel with someone, the more you trust in them.

Hypnosis has done everything for me. It has allowed me to travel the world. Please understand those successes have come from treating everyone who wants me to hypnotize them with respect and empathy.

Chapter 17

Girlfriends-A Blanket Apology

> ***"I'm a little bit wrong***
>
> ***And you're a little bit right."*** *~The Monkees*

I dated a lot. That is putting it kindly. I don't believe in naming names or calling out past loves. There is good and bad in all relationships. I do wish I had been more aware of myself in my younger years, though. Most of the time I was a sitcom character going through the relationship-of-the-week. That young kid I had been, who never thought he would be loved, was desperate to be in a relationship. I would get upset when friends didn't take my relationships seriously or treat them with respect. "Neither do you," they'd reply.

With hindsight, I realize I wasn't ready for a relationship and wouldn't be for an exceptionally long time. I was raised in the Midwest and did not want the Midwest lifestyle. Robert Frost wrote, "I have taken the road less traveled, and it has made all the difference." He never said better or worse, just that it made the difference. So many people enjoy their hometown and the community that comes with it. I did not fully understand how much that was not the life I wanted to live. I was filled with wanderlust and needed to explore the world and try different things. I constantly felt the need to move.

The first problem was that I was more worried about my career than anything or anyone else, including myself and my needs. A girlfriend had no hope of competing with that, nor should she have had to. Relationships don't work when one person is constantly the third or fourth priority for the other. I didn't realize at the time how guilty I was of putting my girlfriends last. I'd cancel plans without a second thought if a show came up.

I also didn't understand how that drive to succeed affected my view of everything and everyone. I wanted everything I did to be perfect. I was always frustrated at myself for not living up to my own expectations.

And I couldn't see past my ideas about what a partner should be to appreciate my partner's individuality. It was like I was looking for a "Stepford" girlfriend who was perfectly equal to every situation, while I was a chaotic mess. I wish I'd had the ability to see the people I dated for everything that was great about them. Instead, I was projecting onto them everything I did not like about myself and hoping they could fix it. That I ever thought it was a valid idea to thrust that onto another person is reprehensible.

Depression will affect every part of a relationship. I didn't have the ability to fully love myself, and I lost my desire to grow, either by myself or with somebody else. I didn't understand that it was the depression making me feel this way. I didn't have the tools to deal with my depression—wasn't aware I needed them. Instead, I inflicted it on the people closest to me. When I felt low, I withdrew, both physically and emotionally, and then complained that no one was there for me. It was a no-win situation. How can anyone be with someone who pushes them away and demands their attention at the same time, especially when they do not even understand they are doing it? My depression made me feel like I was supposed to be alone and isolated.

Compounding the problem was my own compulsiveness. I was always loyal in a relationship, but since I was not ready to be a partner, the relationships didn't work as well for me as flings did. I even gave up on the idea of a girlfriend and just went from hookup to hookup, never realizing when I was hurting someone else. I was careless with a lot of hearts because my compulsions did not allow me to see that others put feelings in where I did not. I hurt a lot of people. I tried to be honest, but never honest enough to prevent heartache.

When I did enter a relationship, it was invariably with a woman who was not really available to me. I would date people who were still stuck on their ex or who were just emotionally unavailable. I think I did that unconsciously to avoid having to commit. Eventually, all the compulsive behavior would come to a head, and I'd reach out for help, but that day was years away.

I wish I could apologize to everyone whose feelings I did not give the consideration they deserved. I wish I could have seen the harm that neglecting their feelings caused. It is easy to say we were not in a relationship. That doesn't mean feelings didn't get involved, and I truly wish I had better respected those emotions.

I learned something from all the women I dated. I wish I had learned some of the lessons faster, but I'm grateful for all the amazing experiences. If my apology means something to you, please know I am sincerely sorry and I wish I had done better. Thank you for being a part of my journey.

Chapter 18

Achieving New Heights on Stage and in Life

"Just one in his life a man has his time
And my time is now, I'm coming alive." *~John Parr*

My goal was always to grow my performing abilities and my career, and often that also meant having to grow and mature as a person. At the age of twenty-one, I was finally able to capitalize on an opportunity that had presented itself three years previously. I'd been doing magic at an event, and an agent from a high-profile agency was attending. The agent really liked my performance and asked me to send them promo material on Monday. I did as he asked, but I didn't hear back. For three years—from age 18 to 21—I sent promo pack after promo pack until finally, around 1996, I got my first booking with them. After that, I began to work for them regularly.

But I had to know why it had taken three years to get a booking. The agent invited me to the office and taught me an unbelievably valuable lesson that would apply both in my career and life.

"You're doing magic," he said walking over to the filing cabinet. He opened the drawer marked *Magicians* revealing dozens of manila folders. "Let's look at your file."

He pulled out every piece of promo I had sent him over the last three years, the first being a letter and a business card. The next was a headshot with info on the back...and so on through ten versions of my promo.

"Let us pretend these are ten different performers. Of these ten, which would you hire for the gigs I send you on?" he asked.

I pointed to the most recent package: a custom folder with stepped promo describing the acts I did and how they fit into an event.

"Exactly. This performer is a professional, not just in his performance, but in his business and presentation. Until you could show me that you took that part of the business as seriously as the performance part, you were not ready."

It was a tough lesson, but at that moment, I really started to learn how to build all the sides of my business and myself. If anyone was going to take me seriously, I had to take myself seriously first. I had to look at myself and see what I was lacking. No one else was going to make me grow. I had to do that on my own or it would never happen.

If I wanted to be professional, I had to act professionally in all aspects of my life.

A year later I was ready to try to build a stronger client base and more money for shows, and I needed a better promo video. I turned to Kim McKinney, an agent friend of mine. I asked him what he wanted out of a video to better sell me to his clients. He invited me to lunch and told me to clear my schedule for the afternoon.

Before lunch, we met in the conference room at his office. Kim had a stack of sample promo videos for me to watch. He held back two and told me to buzz his extension when I was done watching the rest. About an hour later I buzzed him, and he came back with the two other videos. I will never forget what he told me as I watched them.

Pressing Play on the first video, Kim said, "Now this is a great performer. The best. You may be as good one day, but I doubt anyone could be much better. This performer shows up late, argues with clients, and is a pain in the ass. I never book them."

He switched to the second tape. "This performer is mediocre," he said. "You're already better than them. They show up early, they are friendly and easy-going, and everyone likes working with them. I book them all the time."

He then gave me the best words of wisdom of all time:

"If you have the best show *and* you are the easiest to work with, you will always be successful."

In those moments I understood that my character would be the most important aspect of my career. Not my character onstage, but my character as a human being—my integrity. If I treated others with respect, I would get it back in time. If I gave my word and kept it, I would earn bigger and bigger bookings as that reputation spread. If I was a good, honest person with integrity, then quality people would want to work with me.

The people helping me grow were not just agents and bookers. Also entering my life were people who understood the technical, behind-the-scenes part of show business.

David Grossman owns Pegasus Theatrical Supply in Detroit. I first met him and his general manager, also named Kevin, when I was looking for a microphone. To me the store looked like something out of Willy Wonka. They sold special effects lighting, smoke, fog, fireworks, and every sound system imaginable. I had no idea what most of it was. Kevin really took time to go over the different microphones with me to help me find what I needed.

Everyone at Pegasus was like that. They took time with a young guy who could barely afford anything. They taught me what the equipment was and how it worked. They didn't just want to sell me things, they wanted me to understand what I was buying and how it would help me—or not; they also discouraged me from buying things I didn't need.

One time when I went to Pegasus, Dave and Kevin were having an issue with a client. There was an important piece of staging that they needed in Baltimore by morning. I could see the stress the two were under. With no plans for the night, I offered to fly the item out to the client. David's eyes grew wide and the next thing I knew there was $100 in my pocket for food as well as a plane ticket and car reservation waiting for me at the airport.

I did not do it expecting anything in return. I was glad to help because of all the advice they had given me. But that favor was repaid so many times over. After that day, they took even more time with me to explain how to stage a show, how to get the right sound for a particular event. They taught me the importance of assorted styles of lighting.

A lot of work goes into getting better and better in any career. Seek out people who really know their stuff. It is amazing how often they will be glad to offer you guidance if you are willing to listen.

Chapter 19

On My Own and Downhill

> ***"Mama, if that's movin' up***
>
> ***Then I'm movin' out."*** *~Billy Joel*

In 1997, three gigs would end up costing me all the money I had and then some. It started with a month-long gig at the *Detroit Auto Show*. This gig was a huge deal to anyone living in the Detroit area. The auto show was immense. Attendance was always high, and the job paid great money in January when there otherwise was not much work. Unfortunately, the agency that got me the gig would take almost five months to pay me, and by that time, it was an almost negative amount. I was told that I would get paid at the end of the gig, then that I would be paid within thirty days, and finally that I would get paid when the agent got paid. I had to use my credit cards and borrow against the incoming money since I couldn't do any other gigs in that period.

I made two other major financial mistakes at that time, as well.

Please understand this major business philosophy: IF you ever hear yourself say, "I know they screwed over all these other people, but they wouldn't do that to me," know that they are going to do it to you.

I got picked up by a college agency that wanted me to tour the country doing a gameshow at colleges. If I had done homework on the agency, I would have quickly found out how many entertainers refused to work with them and about all the schools that wouldn't book another event from them. I was so eager to pick up gigs I didn't bother, I just jumped in without looking.

The show featured an eight-foot standing cash cube, and the winner had thirty seconds to collect as much money as they could. In hindsight, I can see so many red flags. Had I possessed one ounce of wisdom, I would have backed out at so many points along the way.

First, the deal went from using their vehicle to mine, and it involved the winning money coming out of my pay, not the producers'. It went from a two-man job to just me, with no added compensation. And on and on. My minivan threw a transmission twice on this 10-day run—the first time due to the weight of the cube and the trailer I had to rent to carry it, the second time because the first replacement transmission turned out to be garbage.

The second mistake ended up becoming a benefit to me in the long run.

I was hired to provide entertainers for a nightclub. In total, I brought in eight different performers. These were jugglers, magicians, sideshow clowns, and more to fill a *Dark Circus* club theme. At the end of the night, they gave me a line I had heard from many horrible club owners:

"We didn't bring in as many people as we expected," the club owner would say. "How about we only pay you half the agreed-upon amount."

Many times, I would take that deal, but on that night I couldn't.

"I'm afraid I need all the money to pay the other performers, so I have to get the full payment." I explained.

"Well, if you hold me to that contract, you will never work for me or any of my friends who own clubs in this town ever again," he replied with a smug grin.

I remember the world stopping in that instance: Just like the scene in *The Blues Brothers*, the heavens shined down on me (and as Belushi put it so well, "Jesus-H-Tap-Dancing Christ I see the light") and I said:

"I don't ever want to work for you or any of your crooked friends. I want to work with people who do honest business."

From the moment he paid me, I stuck to that sentence and only worked with people who did legit business. No under-the-table deals—nothing shady. I worked with amazing club owners who ran long-standing clubs with great reputations.

In the middle of all this, I'd gotten back in touch with an old friend from Lili's 21, and he helped me get my first apartment. (Nothing helps being buried in debt like adding a rent bill). At 22, I moved to Downtown Detroit. Rent was ridiculously cheap at that time and even cheaper when you lived in one of the worst zip codes Detroit had to offer. To me, it was paradise.

And yet I knew that even if I ended up homeless, I would not end up anywhere this bad ever again. It was a $100-a-week, no kitchen, tons of bugs studio apartment in the most run-down area of downtown Detroit. On the other hand, the fact that it was downtown—in the middle of everything—was what made it great. The nightclubs, the people, the musicians, and performers were all there. I don't think anyone moves into their dream apartment when they first leave home, but many of us remember it for the first real version of freedom and fun.

Unfortunately, the debt from those three events combined with the cost of moving out put me into horrible financial straits. I ended up deeply in debt. When I look back, it was less than $20,000, but at the time it felt like a million. When you are in debt, it can feel like there is no way out. Eventually, I would make my way to a credit card counselor, who saved me financially. They were able to get my credit card interest lowered and erase late fees and other costs. They set me up on a 7-year plan to get out of debt completely. I'm proud to say I was free and clear in under 4 years.

It took me a long time to really understand some amazingly simple facts:

No one can do everything on their own. True strength is reaching out for help, not keeping it all inside until you break.

Reach out for help when you are overwhelmed. There are always people there to help. There are resources out there for you! You are not the first person to face a difficult problem.

When you reach out to people who *know how to help*, you make things so much easier on yourself. Find that school of fish who know what you need rather than flailing around on your own.

Chapter 20

The Hardest Relationship

> ***"Lean on me***
>
> ***When you're not strong***
>
> ***And I'll be your friend***
>
> ***I'll help you carry on..."*** *~Bill Withers*

For the next few months, I was on my own and having a blast. I met a woman, fell in love, and we moved in together. As relationships often do, this one began to fall apart. We honestly were not happy with each other. We began to argue a lot. I eventually moved into the apartment next door to give us some space as we tried to figure things out. One night we got into a huge argument that ended with me storming out of the building for the night.

I have had to think a lot about how to write about what happened the next day. I considered skipping this chapter completely. But to skip it is to paint an incomplete picture of everything that happened after. To understand me is to understand this event.

The next morning, her best friend had not been able to reach her and was worried, so we decided to go into the apartment to check on her as I had the only other key. We found her body.

After our fight, she had hung herself and died. That image will always be burned into my mind.

In the weeks leading up to this, as we had been arguing, she had threatened to hurt herself. I convinced her to go to community mental health. She made me promise that if she went to therapy, I would not tell her parents. Since she was an adult and getting help, that seemed reasonable. She began seeing a therapist and went on antidepressants. It was not enough.

I wish I had violated her trust and told her parents. That I did not will continue to haunt me. I'll always wish I had done more. I wish I could have handled our last argument better. I wish I could have seen the pain and danger in front of me. I could not.

We called 911. I reached out to my mom and dad, and to Bill and Don. It was all a blur. I remember answering the police officer's questions and finding them ridiculous. They were asking me questions like:

"Where were you last night, and who were you with?"

"What do you two argue about the night before?"

"When exactly did you come home?"

It took me a while to realize that the police had to clear everyone who was close to her. For about two minutes of my life, I was a potential suspect in someone's death. The police were kind and cleared everything up with me very quickly so I could go and be with my family and friends.

Don and Bill stayed close to me for a while after that, constantly checking on me and making sure I was all right. They got me moving when all I wanted to do was sleep and shut down. They gave me room to feel hurt and room to heal.

I went crazy for a long time. My grandfather died shortly after, and I barely remember his funeral. That summer, between my friends and I, we ended up at eight funerals. That entire period is a blur of mixed-up memories and forgotten moments.

I vividly remember the dream I had of her shortly after her death. She was wearing a white dress with a scarf around her neck to conceal the wounds.

"We can be together forever," she said to me.

"No, we can't," I said. "You're dead and I have to move forward."

I never saw her in my dreams again.

I really got lost in my own mind and emotions. The trauma of finding her body along with wondering what I could have done differently was my first thought every morning and my last thought before falling asleep. No matter what else was going on, she was always just below the surface of my thoughts, haunting me.

It is exceedingly difficult for me to piece together most of this. I went to community mental health and got back on antidepressants. I took any gig I could just to stay active. Agents who couldn't find me gigs offered me work as a production assistant on various shows just to keep me busy. Thankfully, friends and family were always there for me and gave me the space I needed to grow and recover.

Bill and Don made sure I was never truly alone and that I always had support. They were constantly planning activities and going with me to gigs. If I needed to break down, they gave me a safe place to break down. When I didn't want to focus on the pain, they would plan other things to do. One of Bill's ideas became a life-changing moment for the better when he and I drove south to New Orleans for the first time.

Chapter 21

Road Trip

> ***"Movin' right along in search of good times and good news***
> ***With good friends you can't lose***
> ***This could become a habit!"*** *~Kermit The Frog & Fozzie Bear*

Bill had decided that what I needed was to get out of Detroit. He was right. I'd always wanted to see New Orleans, so Bill and I hopped in the car, and off we went. We had no big plans or ideas other than scraping up any money we could and heading off on a road trip.

Little did I know how often I would soon be making this drive.

New Orleans was everything I hoped for and more. The food, the sights, and the environment were perfect. We did everything last minute, and yet somehow managed to find a cheap hotel in the French Quarter. We even met people at a magic store who I would stay connected with for years.

As we walked down Bourbon Street that first night, Bill and I got a lot of compliments about the fact that we were, coincidentally, wearing matching dress shirts. After the fourth compliment, I had a realization.

I turned to Bill and asked, "Are you oblivious or just not caring?"

"I guess I'm oblivious. What do you mean?"

"Bill," I pondered, "where are all the women?"

We had arrived during *Southern Decadence*, the large gay pride weekend, which was apparently attended mostly by men. We laughed and went on enjoying this huge party of people having the time of their—and our—lives.

The most important thing we did was go on a ghost tour. What drew me in was not just that the tour promised ghost stories and a walk through parts of the quarter we hadn't seen, but that the guide was a magician as well. It would be a year and a half before I understood how important this tour was, but it was great.

The trip helped me calm down and made me feel better about going home. New Orleans inspired me. It sparked the idea that if I was at the bottom, then it was time to rise higher than I ever had.

Chapter 22

Dave and Buster's

"You wanna be where you can see

Our troubles are all the same

You wanna be where everybody knows your name."

~ Gary Portnoy & Judy Hart-Angelo

While in that ill-fated relationship, I got a gig that would ultimately change my life for the better. I was selected to be the magician at Dave and Buster's in Utica, MI. It paid every week, and I made terrific tips. On top of that, I finished by 10 p.m., so I could do fire shows and magic shows at local nightclubs later in the evenings.

The staff at Dave and Busters were amazing to me. I felt included by everyone and made friends I still have to this day. Even during the breakdown of that horrible summer, the staff was so kind to me. They sent me flowers, checked on me, and supported me even when I was not performing at my best. I have no way of repaying all of them for letting me work through my grief. Once more, I had found a community that lifted me up even when I could barely stand. They helped me swim even when the shark attacking me was in my own mind.

For the first time in my life, I was making *career money*. To me, that meant I knew I had money coming in and I didn't have to take every gig that came my way. I was making $330 a weekend at Dave and Buster's, plus tips, for a total of around $500 a week. Then I could pick up an extra hundred or two doing magic or fire-eating at the nightclubs. *Career money* meant that for the first time, I really felt like I was financially secure.

Because I could now pick and choose my gigs, agents started offering me higher rates so I would say yes. I was learning increasingly more about the "business" side of the business. I was learning that saying no and having a good reason from a business standpoint—made me more valuable.

If I told an agent, "I don't want to do that gig" or "I'm busy that night," I risked sounding arrogant or like I didn't want to work.

But when I could turn down a gig down by saying, "I have a standing show that pays me more than you're offering," I sounded like a professional. Having a business-savvy reason to say no makes people look at you as a businessperson.

I also learned to value my time and my client's time—to learn that showing up early for a gig took the pressure off the agent and the client. The more I put myself into my clients' shoes, the better result I would get. (Again: empathy.) The more I treated my shows like a responsible business transaction, the more shows I got. I learned to treat every gig as the most important gig I had.

My business sense grew—along with my performance skills.

Having a four-hour walk-around-magic gig two nights a week taught me so much about performing. I learned how to build an ice-breaking opening as I approached people. I learned how to make everyone feel comfortable and smile or laugh for a few minutes. I learned to try one new effect a week in the middle of the set to see if I liked it. Eight hours of repeating an effect will tell you whether you want to do it or not.

I started to learn to be myself as a performer. I had a lot to learn about who exactly that person was, but I was beginning to feel more confident about it. I was learning to be less like other performers and projecting my own personality into everything I did. I stopped using other people's scripts and started writing my own material. I began to perform routines based on *me*. This helped me become genuine as a performer. Audiences could tell when I was being authentic and sincere. They responded to that—bonded with that—and I started to feel more comfortable being me.

I could look at myself and see the confidence I was gaining by doing these shows. I could look back at who I had been and see the growth, both as a performer and as a person. I could see the fearless performer who could approach strangers and entertain them. I had come so far from being that scared kid without friends who was terrified of reaching out to anyone. In so many ways it felt like these were two different people: the person of my past and the person I was growing into.

In my heart, I felt that the kid I had been, would be very proud of the person I was becoming.

Chapter 23

A Bigger World Than Just Detroit

> ***"Into the great wide open***
> ***Under them skies of blue***
> ***Out in the great wide open***
> ***A rebel without a clue."*** *~Tom Petty*

The small events I was working on in Detroit were great, but what I really wanted to do was grow my stage career. In Detroit I'd get some stage time at nightclubs, but rarely with the help of agents. Agents knew their clients loved me when I did close-up and walk-around-style magic, but I didn't have the same reputation with my stage show, so they never took the chance.

I made the decision to attend Jeff McBride's Master Class in Las Vegas. Ironically, on my first trip to Vegas, I stayed at the Four Queens. I remember passing the showroom doors each day I was there thinking, "If I could just perform here, all my dreams would come true." How little did I know!

The Master Class would really help me to grow my career. The main instructors were Jeff McBride, a phenomenal stage magician who had performed on stages worldwide before moving to Vegas;

Eugene Burger, one of the most respected close-up magicians and magic philosophers of all time; and Tobias Beckwith, Jeff's manager. There was even a surprise guest speaker: Siegfried of Siegfried and Roy!

That class expanded my life and career in ways nothing in Detroit could have. I learned a lot from all the instructors. Jeff and Eugene would both come to play a much larger part in my life than I could have dreamed of. But Tobias had an immediate impact. Over the next few years, I would send him all my promotional material. He would give me kind but honest feedback and make suggestions as to how I could better sell myself. As a performer, this is some of the most valuable advice you can get. With Tobias's guidance, I would be able to sell myself more effectively throughout my career. Once again, my community had grown.

Oddly enough, that trip to Vegas started me on the path to growing with performers in Detroit. While I had overcome the bullying and abuse I'd experienced in school, it never really left me. Even now, I battle with insecurity. The *cool kids* still give me internal anxiety. It is not their fault or mine. It's an inner mindset I battle. Every time I have reached out to someone I respect; they have been great and become my friends. I just always find it hard to make that reach.

Starting in performing the way I did made it difficult to find communities I was comfortable in. To people on the business side, I was the weird performer. To most performers, I was too successful and business-driven to be looked at as an artist. Most of this was in my own head. It was usually my own insecurities telling me I didn't belong somewhere when I would have been welcomed with open arms.

In a choice between the cool and trendy or the weird and obscure, I would usually choose the latter. I didn't go to the magic store with the flashy advertising, I went to the quiet little shop. That shop was great—it meant the world to me. But by cutting myself off from the other store I denied myself the chance to meet other performers who might have been great guides as well.

Thankfully, Jeff McBride showed me the value of reaching out to others, and I began to embrace that.

Throughout the years, there were two people in the Detroit magic community who were always there to help and push me: Randy Wagner and John Vittorelli. Both had over 10 years on me but were always willing to listen to me and offer advice. They taught me a lot about being a gentleman in business. They'd also call me out when my ego got big.

Together, we created a community of people to build with and grow from. When I was reaching out to invite people to join us, my ego often prevented me from really reaching out. I skipped some people because I saw them as a threat. One of those was a magician so opposite to me it was an odd mirror reflection.

Randy asked me: "Are you not reaching out to Chris because you don't think he has anything to offer, or is your ego just afraid he could outshine you?"

After a second of thought I replied. "You're right. He has a ton to offer. I'll call him now."

Now I was being encouraged to look at it from that angle, I had to make a decision. Could I reach beyond my ego and insecurities? Thank God the answer was yes, or I would not have the deep friendship of *America's Magical Funnyman™* Chris Linn.

Chris's friendship has inspired more than I can put into words. We worked on many shows together, each helping to improve the other. While I was going for edgy and extreme, Chris was geared to fantastic family entertainment. We offered each other new points of view and ideas for delivery. We even put together a dinner theater show for a brief time.

The anxiety and fear in our heads keep us from meeting people we would love to have in our lives. Other people are scary. The voice of that scared kid I once was still lives in my head telling me no one is going to like me. There is no way around that for most of us. It takes a lot of courage to enter a new circle of people. Sometimes it fails. Sometimes it isn't the community we were meant to be a part of. But often, it leads to us being exactly where we need to be.

Chapter 24

Leaving Detroit and Heading Down South

"Oh, c'mon everybody, take a trip with me
Well, down the Mississippi down to New Orleans."
~Gary U.S. Bonds

I had a great base in Detroit. I was making career money and could have made it successfully staying there my entire life. That wasn't what I wanted. I always wanted more—to push my career further. I knew I could make it to *THE BIG TIME* if I could just find the right opportunity.

I did not know what *THE BIG TIME* meant, exactly, but I knew I wanted my name in lights. I wanted to perform in clubs as a headliner all over the country. My biggest dream was to headline in Vegas. I had no idea how to carry out any of that.

Even worse, I started to feel stagnant. I couldn't find anyone who could teach me or show me what to do to perform at the national level. My love life felt like a complete mess, so I was feeling crushed there as well. I really felt adrift; I only knew that I really wanted a change.

Turns out I just needed to take a half step back.

That summer, Don called off his wedding. He was heartbroken. He also had almost two weeks of vacation time blocked off for a honeymoon that wasn't happening. Don had never been to New Orleans. The trip Bill and I had taken eighteen months prior was still fresh in my mind, and I wanted to go back. We loaded up the car and ran down south.

Like most amazing opportunities in life, this next part happened amazingly fast.

While in New Orleans, we decided to take the ghost tour I'd gone on a year and a half earlier. In the intervening time the tour guide I'd talked to previously had sold his business to another tour company. We went on the new tour with the tour operator's girlfriend. She and I chatted throughout, and I told her about my magic and hypnosis acts. At the end of the tour, she introduced me to the tour operator.

"I'd love to have a hypnosis show down here," he said. "With your magic, do you think you could do a séance re-creation as well?"

"Of course, I can," I replied, which sounded better than saying I could fake it for an hour.

I handed him my promo kit. Before the internet, we had to carry our press on us, and I always had a promo kit ready. The tour operator and I talked for the next two months. That August I went back down to New Orleans for a week on my own to finalize our plans. It was an amazingly simple agreement, $750 a week and an apartment in exchange for doing my hypnosis show and a séance re-creation once a day. I would also train as a tour guide to do the ghost and vampire tours as well.

It's scary leaving everything behind. I had an easy life in Detroit with a good circle of friends. This was taking the idea of leaving my comfort zone to the extreme. But as my friends told me, they would always be there, and Detroit would be waiting if I wanted to come home.

I moved down to New Orleans in mid-September 2001. This was quite possibly the worst time to move to a tourist-based city. The attacks of September 11th slowed travel for quite a while. People were afraid to fly, and tourist areas seemed scary. We made the best of it. We did the shows, and I got more stage time. And I became a tour guide.

The ghost tours were a level of performance vastly different from anything I had ever done. The tour guide was handed a large group of people (when I started there was no regulation on the ratio of participants to tour guides) and the streets of New Orleans to keep them entertained. Over two hours we would do a mile-plus walk, stopping every couple of blocks to talk about a haunting that occurred in each spot. If you were good, you could keep the group following you. If you were boring, half of them would leave and go to Bourbon Street. Losing 30% of your tour group was average.

Then something happened that changed that number for me and ultimately changed the industry.

When I started, tour guides dressed as either a campy pirate or a campy vampire. They'd exaggerate their mannerisms and speech to match the costume. Yes, I was guilty as well. Then one night I showed up in jeans and a T-shirt to pick up my paycheck. There were too many participants and not enough guides.

My boss saw me, his eyes lit up, and he said, "You're doing a tour tonight."

"I can't do a tour in street clothes," I told him.

"You're right, it's cold," he said. "Here's a jacket."

Next thing I know, I'm leading a tour. I started by being very honest with my group that night:

"Ever show up to work to get your check and suddenly you're working a shift?"

They laughed and off we all went. I came back with 100% of the participants I started with. Because I was just me, the audience bonded with me and stayed with me.

A light bulb went off in my head.

I called Bill that night after the tour.

"Come out here during your college breaks," I said urgently. "There is a printing press shooting out hundred-dollar bills for guiding these tours and more fun than you can handle."

He chuckled and replied, "See you at mid-term break."

Slowly I was able to get more friends and fellow performers to join me as tour guides. Quickly, the local industry changed. More guides became successful just being themselves. It was a positive change that I'm proud to have been a part of.

The shows lasted for about a year. The tour operator was not a great promoter for the shows, and our relationship became strained. As happens in business, it was time to move on from that tour company. Thankfully, a rival tour company was waiting to add me to their roster.

Sidney Smith is the owner of Haunted History Tours in New Orleans, and he ran his tours very differently. He knew how to have fun, but also how to run the business in a professional manner.

Sidney taught me so much about the business side of a tourist town—how to see that side of things far more clearly and treat it seriously. He also had a hidden heart of gold. I do not know one tour guide who worked for him who ever missed an important bill. He kept guides afloat even when he knew they would never repay the money or the kindness.

I also found a community outside of the performing world that helped me a lot. I'd love to tell you how unique, different, and exotic we all were. In truth, we were that group of friends you need in your twenties. That group of friends who are always happy to see you and always willing to try something new. The group you need to figure out who you really are as a person. One of them summed it up so well by saying, "We all happily listen to each other's bullshit, so no one calls us on our own."

They all believed in my dream. They all believed I could achieve anything I wanted to and be that great headliner I dreamed of being.

There were so many late nights walking around the Quarter, just talking, and dreaming. Most of us found various parts of our dreams. Many years later, I would take my wife to New Orleans with me to show her all my memories. But it was not the same. The place was as beautiful but the people who made New Orleans what it was for me had moved on and become functioning adults with real lives. But there were other groups of idiots roaming the streets, just like we did, and I think there always will be.

One of the magicians I met there helped me grow much more as a performer than I ever thought possible, for several reasons. Warpo is an older street magician. If you ever saw Eugene Levy's character in *A Mighty Wind*, you have seen a version of Warpo. He and I came from vastly different worlds. Warpo is a hippy street magician who also worked at a weed shop when we met. I, on the other hand, have always avoided drugs. We are completely different people, and because of those differences, Warpo could always show me a perspective I could not otherwise see—a point of view I'd never considered. And he always offered it in a kind, gently guiding way.

Warpo also has the best advice for every performer, every time: "Slow down." While some would say he moves too slowly, the truth is Warpo moves with careful deliberation. To him, every word and motion in a performance counts. Even as I perform now, if I feel myself moving or talking too fast, I hear his voice in my mind and smile.

I also began to meet the other New Orleans performers as they came to my show. Meeting them was intimidating, and I braced for conflict. In my experience, many performers tended to berate new performers because they felt they deserved the gig instead. To my surprise, these folks were all incredibly positive and offered valuable critiques to help me improve. There was an attitude of "Be unique, be creative, or don't be on the stage."

None so much as Harry Anderson.

I grew up watching Harry Anderson on *Night Court* and *Cheers*. I devoured every magic event he put on TV. I watched the VHS of his first special, *Hello, Sucker*, until the tape broke. The first time I met him he needed my autograph! The tour operator I worked for was also a wedding officiant. He was marrying Harry and his wonderful bride Elizabeth. To finalize the paperwork they needed a witness, so my boss called me over and I signed the wedding certificate.

This was my first introduction to an idol. I could barely talk to him.

Harry brushed me off a bit at first until my boss gave him my comedy magic demo video. Then the strangest thing happened: He began to treat me as an equal. He offered me friendly advice and always had an open door for me. I wish I had used that door more often. After a great night together writing material, he gave me the best advice of all time:

"Don't try to be the next Harry Anderson or Harry The Hat. Be the first you. Now get out there and eclipse my career."

Unfortunately, at that point I was too insecure to learn as much as I could have. That never stopped Harry from being anything other than kind and giving.

When my parents came into town, Harry made a special point to meet them. I thought I had gushed when I met him, but that was nothing compared to watching my mom fall all over herself. It was hilarious.

Harry had a smile for everyone he met and treated everyone with genuine kindness. Years later, once my hypnosis show had taken off, I wanted to bring it back down to New Orleans. Harry was closing his nightclub there and planning his move to Asheville. He kept his club open two weeks longer than he had planned so I could perform. I didn't know how to say thank you for a compliment that big.

Let us flash forward to 2017 for just a moment. My wife and I would take a vacation in Asheville. She and I got to take Harry and Elizabeth to lunch. It was so great to sit and talk and reminisce. And that I could really say thank you now. At that point I had my show in Vegas, everything was going great, and I could tell him how instrumental he had been in my success. I had no idea he would be gone less than a year later. I can never say enough good things about Harry. The world got a little dimmer with his passing, and I am thankful for the light he shined in my life.

Back to 2002: I was still doing ghost tours for Sidney and those were a particularly important part of my growth as a performer, so I was enjoying them. All the other performers I was meeting were helping me to grow my personal show as well. But of all the people I met in New Orleans, none would be more important than Thom Britton.

Chapter 25

Thom Britton and the Flying Cat Circus

> ***"Just can't wait to get on the road again***
> ***The life I love is making music with my friends***
> ***And I can't wait to get on the road again."*** *~Willie Nelson*

I met Thom at a magic store where normally performers piss on the furniture to mark their territory. Oddly, with Thom and me, nothing like that occurred. Thom had just moved to New Orleans from Birmingham, AL after splitting up from the *Modern Gypsies.* (His partner in that, Michael Saab, would grow Modern Gypsies Productions into an entertainment powerhouse in New York City and beyond.) Thom is an amazing writer, juggler, sideshow performer, speaker, and director. At that moment, he and his fiancée Kristine were settling into New Orleans. Somehow, he and I just started hanging out and writing silly ideas that we figured would never see the light of day. I got Thom a job doing ghost tours, and he thrived at it. We hung out all the time, and I even had the honor of being the officiant of Thom and Kristine's wedding.

As happens with driven performers, we wrote together increasingly more. Then we started writing for a specific audience.

We had talked about writing a show that could tour colleges, and after a year of talking, that show began to take shape. We had the idea of combining magic with sideshow performance. Sideshow stunts were generally about shocking the audience, but we wanted ours to be humorous. Making the audience want to lean in and laugh seemed more valuable than making them cover their eyes and turn away.

We started with an idea called *Freak 'n' Magic*. We made it a 3-person show so we could rotate a third person in and out for extra variety. I called every venue I knew and got us a few dates in the Midwest. This first tour only had about six dates, but it allowed us to start getting videos together and to get busy rewriting after each show. The first thing we wrote was a new name.

The newly named *Flying Cat Circus* was born. We joined the Association for the Promotion of Campus Activities (APCA) so we could start booking colleges. My job in the company, besides performing, was getting the gigs. Thom managed promotional material, website, and marketing. That spring, I got us about a dozen bookings with different colleges in Ohio, Michigan, Illinois, and Pennsylvania. We picked up extra money by promoting my hypnosis show at colleges as well. We would offer the *Flying Cat* one night and the hypnosis show the next for a discount rate. Anything to grow the bookings.

The first thing you learn on tour is that every day you are not doing a show, you are losing money. We even picked up corporate events and bad one-night comedy clubs to keep the expenses down. But we knew that if we really wanted to grow, we needed to get an agent in the college market. In that market, you only want one agent so you're not competing against yourself for gigs. We collected testimonials from every college we performed at to help us get an agent.

Agents turned us down repeatedly.

Every college agent I contacted told me the same thing: "There's nothing like you in the college market. It'll never work."

I finally reached an agent who said, "There's nothing like you in the college market. Wait, there is nothing like you in the college market. Can you send me more info?"

That agent was Greg, owner of the G.G. Greg Agency. A great relationship was about to begin.

Thom and I were ready with the promo. Never call an agent or apply for a job if you don't have your information ready. As soon as we sent it out to him, we started calling colleges we knew to check out Greg's reputation, and he did the same with every college we put on our website.

The first thing he told me about our shows was that we weren't charging enough.

In my ignorance, I told him "We need $900 a show. Charge what you want and can keep everything over the $900."

Greg laughed and said, "I'll be charging more, and I'll just take a standard 30% commission."

In the years to come, Greg could have taken us for a lot of money. He started by billing us out at $1400 a show and consistently got us more money until we were getting $2000 and more for a gig. If Greg had accepted my offer, I would have been shooting us in the foot, and he knew it. Thankfully, he was more concerned with his ethics than making a few extra bucks.

Besides the colleges, Greg also got us booked into more comedy clubs with Thom opening for my hypnosis show. We found ourselves doing APCA showcases to a great response and getting awards and recognition through organizations like Campus Activities Magazine.

We toured for six months out of the year: mid-August through mid-November, then again mid-February through mid-May. One tour had us doing over seventy shows in ninety days! We'd perform, write new material, and review our shows constantly. We constantly pushed each other to improve and get tighter every night.

It was a dream come true: headlining colleges and comedy clubs, then going back to New Orleans where I would pick up my solo corporate gigs, as the magic and hypnosis had been growing for me. The hypnosis was getting as strong as the *Flying Cat*. Working with Thom I really got to develop the hypnosis show I wanted to do. Most hypnosis shows boil down to the hypnotist is a jerk who wants their participants to look like idiots. I wanted a show that said: "I have something fun and interesting to share with you, and if you volunteer, I'll make you look like a star." That really began to flourish.

When I say we did everything together for six months out of the year, I mean it. We traveled in the same van, ate in the same restaurants, worked in the same venue, slept in the same hotel room day after day, for months at a time. (One of the reasons for bringing in the third person was to break up the monotony.)

Thom and I were, and still are, brothers. Brothers argue. We argued a lot. Friends who would see us together would ask me about the bickering and arguing, and I just shrugged it off. But while Thom was great at constructive criticism, sometimes it just felt like criticism. There were private moments that stopped me from ever demonizing this quality about him. The biggest moment that showed me who he truly is was a terrifying day with his wife Kristine.

One day in New Orleans, Kristine had a medical emergency. That, combined with a lack of health insurance and poor medical facilities in New Orleans, meant Thom and I needed to drive her to her family five hours away. Her parents are doctors and were far better suited to help her than a hypnotist and a juggler. On the ride, I saw Thom in full-blown panic mode. While in public he could shrug everything off as a joke; to see someone he loved in pain took up every part of his brain. He had to help however he could. I will never forget that. I never forgot each moment he had my back. I never forgot all the bad relationships he helped me through. And I will never forget that day.

A moment was coming when Thom and I both had to grow. We both had ideas on what we wanted the *Flying Cat* to be, and we were starting to butt heads over it with increasing frequency. Thom was getting more into improv and wanted to move to Chicago. I also needed to make more money. I felt like I was touring and performing just to break even.

Touring colleges was great, but it came with a lot of expenses. Most tours I'd only end up a couple grand ahead of where I started, at best, with at least a few months until the next tour. The ghost tours, while fun, supplied me enough money to survive but not to grow.

I needed to figure out a way not only to survive but to thrive in my career. I hated living week to week. Friends made sure I did not have to have sleep for dinner. They could see when I was low and always offered a kind hand. But I needed a plan.

I was getting more private gigs in the Midwest. The touring and being in New Orleans had increased my reputation and created bit of a demand. Also, dead seasons for colleges and ghost tours were a fun time to work comedy rooms throughout the Midwest.

In 2005, as I approached my 30th birthday, I produced a plan. I would live part-time in New Orleans, part-time in Detroit, and part-time on the road with the *Flying Cat*. This way I could work the college gigs, work the corporate and college gigs in the Midwest, and do ghost tours in New Orleans when my schedule was open.

Something much bigger was waiting for me than I could have ever imagined.

Chapter 26

My 30th Birthday Present to Me

> ***"And the course of a lifetime runs***
> ***Over and over again…***
> ***But the mother and child reunion***
> ***Is only a motion away."*** *~Paul Simon*

Moving back to Michigan part-time gave me an idea for my 30th birthday. While financially I was not doing as well as I wanted, I was doing well enough to be able to live my dreams. I was touring and making money at it, seeing the country, and doing what I loved. I was, and am, very thankful for my life. The more I reflected on my life the clearer it became that I wouldn't have everything I had if my birthparents had not given me up for adoption. I also realized that having kept me for five months there had to have been some kind of bonding. I decided to look for my birthparents.

I talked to my mom and dad first, as I wanted their blessings. They were both incredibly supportive. I had only one main concern that I needed to address. I needed to know that my parents had never known or introduced me to my birthparents. My only fear was finding out they had known my birthparents all along and had hidden it from me. There are so many stories of the birthparents being *Auntie Brenda* down the street or *Uncle Lou*, who you'd see every year or two. I was afraid that my birthparents were an active part of my life, and I was unaware. That would have felt like a massive betrayal. Thankfully, Chuck and Rosemary didn't know who my birthparents were, either. I'm glad to know that my mom and dad never tried to hide things from me.

Catholic Social Services of Michigan oversaw my adoption, so that's where I started. Thankfully, my birthmother had chosen to keep the adoption records open. I learned that her name was Annette and that my birth-father's name was Howard. It was so strange to have names after almost 30 years. I read all the information she'd left me about herself and my birthfather. She'd left a letter of love explaining that she did not have the ability to raise me properly.

I decided to find her first. It was almost impossible.

I followed every lead I could based on her letter and any information I could find online. I paid for search services and hit dead end after dead end. But when I went back to the records, I found one line that changed everything; it said at the time of my adoption, my mother had a sister who was twenty-one and a nurse.

Through online searches, I traced my aunt's life from being a nurse, to becoming a doctor, to earning a business degree, to running a hospital in Washington. I left a message on the only office number I could find for her. Her assistant called me the next morning with some odd questions. I guess having someone ask me odd questions is proper when I am asking for something so odd as looking for my birthmother. After a few minutes, the assistant said she would call back if she had any other information for me. Less than an hour later, my birthmother called.

She was gushing at once. We talked for hours. She was living in California at the time, newly married, and had two children. I had siblings! Annette had done some incredible things with her life. She was a great painter and poet who loved to sing. She had been a radio DJ and had toured as a backup singer for Bob Seger. Growing up, she came from a toxic home where she, her two sisters, and their mother had to endure a lot of abuse. Giving me up was the best thing she thought she could do for me. It was easy to hear the guilt in her voice. It was even easier to hear the relief when I told her of the life I have because of her choice to give me up. We talked and talked. She even made plans to meet me in Michigan.

After hanging up with her, my Aunt Corrine called me. She'd wanted Annette to talk to me first, then got permission to call me as well. I was so blown away by my aunt and her life. She had really taken a diligent path to amazing success. She told me about my other aunt, Sabrina, and my grandmother, Barbara. She even fleshed out the story of my adoption. My mother had been too young to put me up for adoption, and her abusive father wanted to keep me. Behind her parents' back, my Aunt Corrine became my birth-mother's legal guardian so I could be put up for adoption. I cannot even imagine the courage it took to pull that off.

I met Annette that next week in person. Unfortunately, Annette was an alcoholic, and it was extremely apparent during that first visit. While she tried holding it together, her drinking got worse as the night went on. After too many drinks, it was clear she did not want to know about me. She wanted to know about the son she'd imagined I would have been. She had an idea of who I was supposed to be and was trying to fit me into that idea. Meeting her was tough.

We still talked on the phone here and there after that first meeting. About a month after our visit, my Aunt Corrine called me. She asked if I wanted to come to Texas for a big family gathering where I would be able to meet my siblings, grandmother, cousins—everyone. I could tell that she knew Annette had a problem without her actually saying as much, and she did her best to make it clear that I would be in a larger, safer environment. I was glad to go.

It was a wonderful time. I got to meet so many people. My half-sister made a quick appearance before ducking out to run an errand. This was the most blatant case of walking in, sizing me up, then immediately calling her friends to talk about me. My cousins Emily and Brianne are amazing. My grandmother was sweet and extraordinarily strong. My Aunt Sabrina and her husband Jeff were filled with love. All of us had a wonderful time. My community had grown again.

Alcoholism does not just go away, though. A few years later, as it often does without help, the disease of alcoholism took her life when Annette committed suicide. Sadder still, her funeral was the first time all three of her children were in the same room together. Having been through a suicide death before allowed me to bring some temporary comfort to her son and daughter, my brother Seth and sister Celeste.

Annette's death sent Seth down his own path of addiction.

The following Thanksgiving turned into an intervention. Seth had ended up in jail and agreed to get help. Thanks to my friend Bill, Seth was admitted into Bridge House, a 1-year recovery program in New Orleans. Seth had no idea that the clinical director was my best friend. Bill kept an eye on Seth and never cut him any slack. While there have been a few bumps on Seth's journey, I am so proud of the sober life he lives and how he continues to grow each day. Maybe that is why I came into his life: to offer a light in a dark time.

To have them all as extended family is amazing to me.

After locating my mother, I went looking for my birthfather, Howard. My friends, what happened next is so unbelievable it could only happen in real life!

Chapter 27

There Are No Coincidences

> ***"I see friends shaking hands***
>
> ***Saying how do you do***
>
> ***They're really saying I love you."*** *~Louis Armstrong*

My birth records listed my birthfather as Howard B. Goldman. I found two in the Detroit area. The first took my call and when I explained I was looking for my birthfather, told me he never had kids. One down and one to go. I found phone numbers first for Howard's mother, my grandmother, and had a brief conversation with her. Then I found his phone number and called him.

His wife answered the phone. I didn't know whether she knew about me or not, so I played it safe. All I told her was that I was looking for my birthmother and that Howard might have information on her. Howard's wife Lori was truly kind. I told her I would be up late for work, and he could call me anytime. He called me that night as I was setting up for a gig.

Once again, I made it clear that primarily I was looking for information on my birthmother so as not to put him on the spot. When asked if he knew her, he confirmed he absolutely knew her and knew why I was calling. Oddly enough, most birthparents are terrified they are being contacted out of resentment. I quickly made it clear I was calling to thank him—that I was living a great life thanks to a hard decision he and Annette had made, and I wanted to express my gratitude. I also had questions for him, and we began to talk. Howard told me about his success in a number of different businesses from mortgages to medical supplies. Then he asked me what I did for a living, and everything changed.

I explained to Howard that I did hypnosis and magic, touring the country. With the most quizzical sound in his voice, he asked me to repeat myself. I immediately assumed I was going to have to justify my career path. It was just the opposite. Howard's hobbies since childhood had been magic and hypnosis. I was living his version of the road less traveled. We talked for hours about different performers along with exchanging stories about each other's lives.

We decided to meet a few weeks later at a public show I was doing.

I do not get nervous backstage. I was doing my hypnosis show at the Improv Inferno in Ann Arbor. Howard and Lori would be in the audience that night. I was nervous and pacing the floor before showtime. Everyone in the improv troupe knew that Howard was coming, and one of them asked me the funniest question I had ever been asked:

"Do you think your birthfather will recognize you?"

"You mean when the music hits, the voice-over starts, and I walk out onstage? Yeah, I think he might have a clue."

I remember clearly finding his face in the audience. I remember being nervous—even more so when his wife Lori volunteered. I made it through a good show, and the three of us went to dinner and talked all night. We made dinner plans for the following week. Those dinners became increasingly frequent lunches.

Howard and I started off as just two guys getting to know each other. No expectations, no wants, just learning and enjoying each other. Because of that, our relationship grew and grew quickly. We were becoming friends and even building toward being family.

Within a few months, we took a trip to Chicago together. Howard was a huge fan of Eugene Burger (my Master Class instructor). I got us a weekend of private magic lessons from Eugene. It was a great bonding experience, and the bond kept growing.

It took me a while to see the family genetics. It was months before I really saw his profile and noticed how similar we looked. Especially when, at that same moment, I watched him run his hands through his hair in the same exasperated way I would. I really lost it one day driving with him, when after a frustrating day he was complaining while scratching his nose nonstop—the exact same tick I have always had when feeling the same way.

As great as it was meeting Howard, meeting his daughter Cate was terrifying.

Seeing Cate for the first time knocked all the wind out of me at once. I saw it. For the first time, I saw someone who looked like me. She even had other similarities to me. Her speaking pattern, the inquisitive look in her eyes, all the different ways she presented herself seemed so familiar to me. She blew me away. She was seven turning eight. It took everything I had not to start crying, but I didn't want to throw myself at her. At that moment, she didn't know who I was, and it wasn't my place to tell her. Yet we became close, talked often, and she'd invite me to dinners and events. I was there for her as much as I could be and made time for her even when I was busy.

Howard had a son, Ben, from his first marriage. Ben was eleven years younger than me and didn't know about me until I contacted Howard. It took Ben a while to get comfortable with the idea of me. For a 19-year-old growing into his adult life, I was an odd concept to have thrown into the mix. Ben really put in an effort, and I made myself available for it. Slowly we grew close as well. I am so proud to have him as a brother. I see a lot of me in his artistic side and his fearlessness to tackle challenges.

Howard and Lori had accepted me into their family, and it filled me with joy. Lori opened herself to the situation with nothing but love in her heart, going as far as to tell people after meeting me that no one could ever have enough family, and she was thankful I was now a part of theirs.

I felt so much a part of the family that I wanted Howard and Lori to meet my mom and dad. The idea sparked nervousness on everyone's part, but everyone agreed it would be wonderful, and so we planned a dinner. I was excited and not nervous at all—until I got to the restaurant parking lot. I was with my mom and dad. Howard and Lori were waiting at the restaurant. I got scared and almost froze. I started worrying, thinking about my mom's brassy attitude.

Mom, the one person in the world who can embarrass you like no other person can and who seems to thrive on embarrassing us at different moments. I was terrified of the first meeting, but I didn't need to be.

Rosemary and Howard locked eyes from across the room and immediately embraced with tears in their eyes. They thanked one and other for both bringing me into the world and raising me. Rosemary, Lori, Chuck, and Howard all instantly fell in love with each other. It was a night of laughter and joy.

Once again, my heart was full, and my community had grown.

All of this happened in 2005. I didn't know that as my family was building in Michigan, I was about to lose everything in New Orleans.

My plan had been to split time between Detroit and New Orleans; then Hurricane Katrina struck. No one had any idea what was coming. I am thankful I was in Detroit, as I would not have evacuated. Before Katrina, my friends and I threw hurricane parties. After the devastation of Katrina, most everyone I knew had lost most of what they had. The second level of my condominium complex flooded; I had a first-level unit. Everything I had in New Orleans was gone but everyone I loved was safe. I lost things and not people. I was sad but thankful.

As Katrina was happening, my friend John-John took me out. A local bar was charging a cover to raise money for Katrina victims. Upon giving the bouncer my New Orleans ID, he tried to give me the money they collected. A kind gesture to be sure. Instead of taking the money, I gave him a list of charities in New Orleans that I knew would be helping people in need. It looked like I would be in Detroit full-time for now.

Howard also had a plan. His ability to see opportunity is only surpassed by his ability to weed out bullshit. His business sense is amazing. He owned multiple companies, including medical and chiropractic supplies, and was looking for a new way to get exposure for the companies. He also felt I could be doing bigger things with my talents, and he started working on a plan that would take my career to a new level. The idea was simple: offering my show as headlining entertainment for different trade shows in exchange for booth space.

Thom and I found a replacement for me on the Flying Cat's next tour, and I started working with Howard. The response was amazing. Major trade shows across various industries were glad for the free show and happily provided Howard's company with a booth. Howard made me a salaried position. Everything began to take off.

The first thing that grew was my ability to focus on the show. I was not worried about the next gig; I could concentrate on growing the hypnosis show into exactly what I wanted it to be. I also got to talk to all the directors of the tradeshows when we booked them. I learned what they needed out of a show and how to deliver that. I began to understand the meaning of spheres of influence.

Spheres of influence says that If I call you without you knowing me you will not return my call. If I call you and leave a message saying someone you know told me to call, I'll get a call back. With all the tradeshow directors knowing other directors, we booked shows steadily. Things were going great and only getting better.

These shows put me in front of executives and successful businesspeople all around the world. I had the opportunity to not only perform in all fifty states but to visit new countries and cultures. Spain, Puerto Rico, Mexico...my experience grew exponentially.

A couple of years into all of this, Howard and Lori were expecting a new baby. Within a week or so, we learned they were expecting twins. Soon after, the final verdict came in: triplets. All of us were excited.

As Cate was turning ten, Howard decided it was time to tell her everything about me. Cate was born with a natural ability to be exceedingly kind yet keep people at arm's length. Howard always found it surprising that she became close with me from day one.

Had I been part of the conversation when Howard told her who I was, she may have never made it to ten! Here's how Howard told me it went down:

Cate: Kevin can't be my brother!

Howard: Why not?

Cate: Well, aren't you two the same age?

Yes, had I been there, I'd have killed her for that!

Cate and I went to lunch the next day while she was processing the information. This kind of news is a lot for anyone to handle, especially a ten-year-old. We decided on a simple solution: While she was processing having a new brother, she could just be happy that she had a best friend in me who would always be there for her.

Lori spent months five through seven in a hospital bed preparing for the triplets' birth. Her patience and perseverance blow me away to this day. I was there the day that Ellie, Sam, and Grace were born. It was the day I learned love can never be divided, only multiplied.

I love all three of them with all my heart. I remember looking at them and saying "Welcome to your life, there's no turning back. Elizabeth, I am your brother, I love you, and I will always be there for you. Grace, I am your brother, I love you, and I will always be there for you. Sam, I am your brother, I love you, and I will always be there for you. I will try to protect you from your sisters, but good luck!"

I talk a lot about how people came into my life and built my community, helping to shape who I became. I knew with these three, it was my duty to help shape them.

Chapter 28

The Comedy Castle

> ***"If life seems jolly rotten***
>
> ***There's something you've forgotten***
>
> ***And that's to laugh and smile and dance and sing."*** *~Monty Python*

The show was growing rapidly, along with my reputation as a dependable performer who people wanted to work with. I was doing enough shows that I could gauge what the audience was embracing. On the weekends when I didn't have a corporate show booked, I would be at different comedy clubs trying out new material.

During this time, I also got one of the best opportunities of my life.

Mark Ridley is the owner of the *Comedy Castle* in Royal Oak, Michigan—one of the top comedy clubs in the nation. The first time I called the *Comedy Castle* to ask about doing the open mic, I was 18 years old. Somehow, I got Mark on the phone. He told me I was welcome to do the open mic, but if I tried to drink, I would be banned forever. An easy deal for me.

I worked up from performing at open mics to becoming an emcee, a job that taught me how to get the audience's attention and keep their focus on the stage. I also learned how to make the acts I introduced sound special and exciting. This resulted in more performers wanting to work with me. All the while, I would send Mark every bit of new promo I could. He was kind enough to give me advice and guidance, and shared my video and info with other agents, which led to more gigs. After a couple of years, he thought I was ready to be a feature: the middle act on a bill. This helped me work more closely with more comics and learn the craft of getting laughs.

While he had booked me regularly as a feature act doing my comedy magic, by 32 I knew I was ready to headline with my hypnosis. But Mark didn't think hypnosis would work in his club. He'd had bad experiences with hypnotists over the years and just didn't feel comfortable booking a hypnosis show. I made the point that he knew me. I pointed out that he knew I would never do anything to hurt an audience member. I promised I would fill the club even on an off night. But the biggest promise I made, the promise that sealed the deal, was this:

I told him if the show didn't work out, I would never bring it up again.

That got a yes out of him.

My hope was that Mark would love the show and want to book it yearly. After my first hypnosis show at the Castle, he offered me multiple dates throughout the year. Mark and the staff at the *Comedy Castle* still give me the greatest of honors by letting me pick dates that coincide with my yearly trips to Michigan. Everyone at the Castle makes it a special show, and I am always honored to be there.

Chapter 29

Inspiration Into a Larger World

> ***"Do you wanna go big or not?***
>
> ***This might be our final shot***
>
> ***Do you wanna just give in or give it everything we've got?"***
>
> *~The Mighty Mighty BossToneS*

In 1993, I was incredibly lucky to meet someone who would be a huge inspiration—someone far more successful than I could imagine being at the time. His kindness and generosity improved my career and made me a better person.

As a high school graduation present from my friend Mike, I got a ticket to the *Mighty Mighty BossToneS* concert. It blew my mind. The volume, the energy, and all the good vibes. People in a mosh pit not trying to hurt anyone, just having fun and partying together. A community coming together for a fun night.

Onstage I saw a performer and band who gave every ounce of energy and sweat they had. I watched the singer, Dicky Barrett, sing, dance, crowd surf, and interact with the audience like it was a roomful of friends he had known his entire life. The performers I knew at the time, for lack of a simpler description, wanted to be Dean Martin. They wanted to be low-key and cooler than the room. Here was a person doing just the opposite. He was not above the crowd; he *was* the crowd. He was everyone in the audience, and he gave all his energy to every one of them. That's what I wanted to do. It would take me years to get there, but he showed me a blueprint I didn't even know existed.

After the show, I was able to talk to Dicky for a few minutes as he walked among the crowd interacting with people. Everyone I knew who went to the show has a memory of someone in the band talking to them. He showed me how every single person is important to a show and a career—that treating people with respect made a real impression. When the band came to town next time, Dicky saw me doing magic for some friends of mine, and we talked more. This continued every time they came into town and led to a friendship that has always been an amazing help to me. I could always ask Dicky for information on performing. I also learned a lot just by watching him and how he interacted with fans. In many ways, he became a role model for the performer I wanted to be. Even though he would always be cooler as a rockstar than I would be as a hypnotist!

It means so much to see someone who is succeeding doing a version of what you want to do and have them believe in you and offer you friendship. When starting on the path to any dream, it is so easy to feel discouraged by all the challenges and frustrations. To have someone you believe in believe in you is a gift that keeps you motivated through the tough times.

In 1995 I got to perform on the third stage of *Lollapalooza* in Detroit and the *BossToneS* were on the main bill. Dicky made it a point to stop by my show. After the show, we went and watched the second stage acts on that rainy Saturday. I still laugh remembering the women standing in front of us talking about the cute singer from the *BossToneS* with no clue that the person in the poncho behind them was that very cute singer. When the band on the second stage ended, Dicky took off his poncho, messed up his hair, threw on some sunglasses, and was Dicky Barrett. For the next couple of hours, he sat there signing autographs and taking pictures with everyone.

Around 2007, Dicky came to a corporate event I was doing in L.A. It was an amazing experience to have someone I respected watch me do what I do best. But it didn't stop there. After the show, Dicky invited me to Sarah Silverman's birthday party. My brain at this point shut down and went to automatic mode, as thinking would have only screwed me up. I met some of the greatest people there—people I'd seen on TV and in movies just chilling out and having fun. Dicky asked me to do magic for some of them, and it was my greatest pleasure to entertain people who have entertained me for years. I was walking on air before, during and after my "A-List Hollywood Party" experience. Upon reflection, I see it differently now though. I cannot change it in my mind to the wild party I would love to talk about. I can't tell you about my amazing hook-up that night because it never happened.

What did happen was that my world got bigger. Dicky led me to the start of a new level in the dream I get to live. I saw the next steps on the path to growing my career to where I want to be. He showed me that just like him, all these stars were people. Real people. People who put in the work, people who made sacrifices to get where they were, but people. It showed me that I could do that too. I could be that if I wanted to put in the work and make it happen.

As I tried to push for another level, I would abuse my friendship with Dicky. My compulsive behavior led me to treat a lot of people in ways I should not have, including him. Once I got help, I appreciated his forgiveness. As always, he provided me with insight that helped me keep growing.

Dicky said that when we first spoke, he knew I would make it. He told me he was proud of me for getting to where I was. Thanks to Dicky, I always had a positive thought to push through demanding times.

Thank you, Dicky, for all the inspiration.

Chapter 30

The Filming

"You've got to know when to hold 'em

Know when to fold 'em

Know when to walk away

And know when to run." *~Kenny Rogers*

I had a plan to get on the national scene. I was going to film a show and sell it to a broadcast company. The main goal was to film it to industry standards then sell it to *Comedy Central* or even buy the time on a network and air it myself. I talked with people at local networks and knew the chance I had to take. I had to film it myself and then sell it myself. No one had tried something like this with hypnosis and I wanted to give it a shot.

I found a great venue with a club I had performed at for years and got management's blessing to use it. I had to hire a production company that could film up to modern television standards and another to edit everything together properly. This would cost about everything I had.

I was also dating someone who helped me put this all together. Unfortunately, it was a painful relationship and an even more painful break-up. This was an unhealthy relationship where I allowed myself to be treated dismally. I stayed long after it was worth staying because I had a need to win—to prove I could make a broken relationship healthy. All I proved is how much pain I could cause myself.

I cannot explain how foolish I was to let a huge project fall into nothing. But I could no longer be attached to it and that relationship. I didn't move with the video in any of the ways I should have. I let myself down, and I know I let other people down as well.

I did not understand my emotions. My compulsive need to be right and to win was starting to take increased control over my life. I couldn't take time to process my emotions, I just acted on them. I was with someone emotionally manipulative to me, and I let it go too far. I let her hurt me and I took that hurt out by abandoning something that could have been an enormous success.

I was not ready to understand the flaws in me that let myself get into—and stay in—a relationship like that. I was not ready to face my behavior. The bottom was getting close for me, I just didn't know it yet. I was spending more and more time at casinos. I was having more flings and fleeting relationships. I could never allow myself to feel comfortable.

A crash was coming.

The upside to all of this was that I did end up with the greatest hypnosis promo that was available at the time. That video showed a level of professionalism that was second to none. Any gig I pitched that video to, I got the booking. It filled my performing calendar. I just wish I had not disappointed myself and others by not achieving what it could have been.

Chapter 31

Moving to Vegas

"There's a feeling I get

When I look to the west

And my spirit is crying for leaving." *~Led Zepplin*

In the beginning of 2010, I created the opportunity to move to Vegas. H&H and CBG, Howard's companies, had plenty of events they wanted a presence at. Having someone out there through the spring and fall to represent them was a valid plan. I researched every trade show worth being at. I searched through all the short-term, furnished apartments near the convention center and was lucky enough to find a great one. I was getting everything I ever wanted. The chance to be in Vegas to learn and experience all of it.

I blew it big.

It's ironic that I moved on April Fool's Day 2010. I left Detroit with all the luggage I could take on Delta and had my car shipped. I wasn't feeling well when I got there; my arm was sore for some reason. Unpacking in my new apartment, the pain in my arm got so bad I spent my first night in Vegas in the E.R. with a staph infection. But within a few days, I settled into a town where I knew no one—though I did know where the casinos were!

And for that month, casinos were all I did during my downtime. I met gambling friends, and we played table and card games every night. Thankfully I still fulfilled all my convention work, though not as well as I could. Life became long days and longer nights of gambling. I never played slots because I thought those were for suckers.

Turns out, I was the sucker. A compulsive gambler never wins, they just get a temporary loan that they will give back very soon. Every time I won, I lost my winnings within a day or two. I had started down the slippery slope.

"I'll only gamble with the cash on me, not with my ATM card."

"I'll only go to the ATM, but I won't do cash advances on my credit card."

"I'll only do cash advances on my credit card, but I will not open a line of credit with the casino."

The goalposts for what I would or would not do shifted constantly as my losses mounted.

My last week gambling, I played all I had. Every dime. I didn't enjoy playing anymore, but I had to win. I didn't feel like my career was succeeding. I didn't believe I'd ever get the opportunity to be the headliner I wanted to be. I thought if I could win enough at the casino, I could buy my celebrity.

I felt that I couldn't earn my own show, but that a casino would be so impressed with my gambling skills they'd be eager to give me a showroom. I had to prove I was smarter, stronger, better than the casinos—casinos that got bigger and bigger every year because of all the money they took in.

I played until I had nothing left. Nothing in my pocket and nothing in my soul.

With Dad being in A.A., I knew there was help available. I also knew I had spent my entire life making sure I never did anything that would land me in those meetings. It was not just the gambling that broke me, though. After the failure to launch with the TV filming, I kept concentrating on the horrible relationship that had made me bury it. With every bet I made those last few days, this voice in my head kept nudging me:

"Doesn't this feel like when you two were fighting?"

"This feels a lot like when she hurt you again."

"Didn't you want to get away from her, just like now?"

I started seeing more clearly every compulsive thing I was doing or had done. It was not just the unhealthy relationship with that ex, it was every bad compulsive decision I'd made in every relationship. I saw every mistake I'd made by instantly jumping on an emotion instead of facts. I saw all the mistakes I'd made and was likely to keep making. I saw arguments with friends and time wasted.

At that moment, I was sick and tired of being sick and tired.

Chapter 32

Hi, My Name is Kevin, And I Am A Compulsive Gambler

> ***"It's amazing***
>
> ***when the moment arrives***
>
> ***that you know you'll be alright."*** *~Aerosmith*

April 29, 2010, was my last bet, and April 30th was my first meeting. Even my gambling friends had told me I needed to get help. When I told them I was going to a meeting, they did something very unexpected: They paid off my marker at the casino we played at. A marker is a debt/check you take out with the casino, and it must be paid in full within 30 days. In Nevada, markers are classified as a check, so bouncing a marker is like bouncing a check. A federal crime. My gambling friends took my last $200 and told me they ran it up to $3500. The amount I needed to clear my marker.

The pit boss at the table told me a different story: These guys paid it off themselves. They decided if I was going to get help, they would make that part easier on me—easier than it should have been. They reminded me it's important to show compassion for someone who is down but willing to get help.

Telling your friends and family you need help is a terrifying prospect. A friend of mine starts off an addiction lecture with the line: "No one knows you better than you know yourself. If that is true, why were you the last to know you had a problem?" Upon telling my friends, they had to call each other to find out who bet on closest to May of 2010. Ever notice all your best friends are assholes?

But truly, most of my friends knew I had a problem, and everyone stepped up to find out what I needed. I remember being fourteen when a family member of mine had a drug problem. He was sent to a rehab facility on the beach in Hawaii. I told everyone I needed that. Everyone said no. They would not send me to Hawaii, but they would support me going to meetings and be an ear to listen to. Well, Hawaii had not helped my family member with his problems, so I couldn't be that mad that I had to do it at home.

No one walks into their first meeting happy. Everyone comes in after they have lost everything. They walk in thinking that G.A. has ways that you can get your money back. They do not. But they have the tools to help you not lose anymore.

I was sitting in a folding chair, crying in front of a group of strangers who knew me better than I knew myself at that moment. I was surrounded by people who had been there and got better. People who understood how my head was racing nonstop. They told me there was a way to stop all that. In what they told me I realized a profoundly serious truth about myself: I was not just Kevin the Compulsive Gambler. I could've shortened it to I am Kevin, and I am Compulsive.

I began to see how my compulsive desires pushed people away and pushed me farther away from my goals. I realized that if I could cure the symptoms of gambling, I could work on curing the disease that was my compulsive behavior.

The rest is no big secret: I did the work.

G.A. helped me change so many things. It really helped me become a better adult and person. I learned why I procrastinated and would overbook myself. I learned why I avoided certain confrontations and went looking for others. I met people who understood me and have helped me grow.

I meet a lot of people in these meetings, from every walk of life from CEOs to entertainers to Suburbanites, the pillars of the community, and the destitute. All were there to achieve that functioning mindset and help each other do the same. I gave my 30-day keychain to my dad. If it had not been for his influence, I do not know that I could have taken that first step. The year keychain means so much; it's a symbol of all the growth I have achieved. That growth means everything. I have been able to give back and aid others in the program. The most important thing I can say, being gambling free since April 30th, 2010, is actually pretty simple:

IF YOU NEED HELP, GET HELP!

The help is out there. People you have never met are waiting to offer friendship and help you to get better.

Chapter 33

The Beginning of an Amazing Adventure

> ***"There's not a word yet,***
>
> ***For old friends who've just met."*** *~Gonzo, The Muppets*

The G.A. community also led to another: One of the performers in a meeting told me about a Friars Club gathering: A Friday night get-together among entertainers after their shows. I was excited. It was time to join that community, as well.

My first time attending a Friars Club meeting was yet another night that changed my career and my life. It is always hard to step out of your comfort zone, but any growth I have ever experienced came from leaving that zone. As an unknown performer, it is intimidating to think of walking into a room where you are the stranger in town and everyone else has a similar skill set. You wonder what value you can bring to the group and whether you will be accepted.

Everyone was great. I got to see Vegas as a community of performers—a community of people who were building each other up. I saw headliners, middle acts, and touring performers all getting together to offer advice and friendship. I felt welcomed and was grateful to be a part of it. Without the Friars Club, I might never have met some of the most important people in my life in Vegas.

Bizzaro, the magician in black, was someone who spoke my language. We communicated in movie quotes and half-jokes and understood each other right off the bat. A brilliant inventor, Bizzaro would end up redesigning a magic trick I created for other magicians into a much better product. Every project I worked on; he could make it look better instantly. His abilities as a writer, director, performer, and friend helped me through a lot of challenging times. I wish all of you could meet him or see him perform. He makes your life better by being in it.

Penny, who might well be the kindest person this world has ever produced, is one of the greats. She's a fantastic stand-up performer and writer in many popular Vegas shows. Her desire to know everything about people she meets might be terrifying if it was not so genuine. Her ability to connect people, build people up to others, and create friendships makes her one of the most known and loved people in Vegas. She deserves all that love and more.

Thanks to Penny I would meet Alex, another great friend who has always been there for me and has built every showroom I have been in, in one way or another. He's the one person I know with the skills to save your butt when you have a problem.

I'm trying to avoid name-dropping in this book. I mention these people because they are true friends and deserve credit for growing my life and my dreams. But there is one name I must drop. Not because of his celebrity, but because he influenced my career before I ever met him. He would grow to become a big brother and one of my dearest friends. Plus, he was a Detroit native who made good, not just in Vegas but worldwide. My life got so much bigger the day *The Amazing Johnathan* walked into my life.

I blew my first meeting with him. I gushed. Seriously, total fanboy. Not the best way to introduce yourself as a professional. But we talked a little, and with Penny working in his show, we ran into each other frequently. Eventually, we met for lunch. He later told me he was shocked that I picked up the check. Apparently, people tended to expect him to pay for everything because he was more successful.

A friendship was born. We would even end up performing in the same theater when I got my Vegas career-break months later—The Amazing Johnathan in the big theater, and me in the smaller one next door.

I often say that in Vegas, my heroes became people and some of those people became friends. Johnathan is who I think of every time I say that. Every lunch, every text, every adventure, and bad joke we shared is such a part of me. He helped me embrace silliness when I got too serious. He allowed me the space to talk about joys and troubles and everything in between. And he had no problem sharing mistakes he'd made and offering me guidance on ways to avoid the same.

Once again it's an uplifting feeling when someone you believe in believes in you, not just as a performer but as a friend. He included me in so much and was such a dear friend. His mother was always so sweet, and the victim of a lot of his practical jokes. Anytime she attended a show, Johnathan would introduce her as *Nevada's #1 drug dealer* or *The oldest stripper in Las Vegas*. When Johnathan and I were both in Detroit at the same time, we would spend time together with his mom. She would even come to my Detroit shows with her family. She was always full of love and laughter. I was the guest on Johnathan's video podcast *Burn Unit*, and after she watched it, she told me it was her favorite episode because it just felt like two friends sharing and hanging out. I loved that I could be friends with this person who had so much more to offer than just the persona that was *The Amazing Johnathan*.

He had no chance of remembering meeting me in a tiny comedy club around 1999. I had just done a show the week earlier that I thought was going to crush my career. A smoke machine I used—which exhaled a huge billow of smoke when I walked on stage—followed by a fire-eating set was too much for the smoke detection system to handle. The fire alarm went off and the fire department shut down my show for 20 minutes.

Johnathan said, "I did a show in a rotating showroom on the top level of a 73-floor building. My smoke machine started the alarm, stopped the room from spinning, and shut down the elevators for almost two hours."

"You'll be fine," he told me.

In Las Vegas, there were three big moments when Johnathan positively impacted my career. The first was when I asked him to come watch my show and give me his opinion. At the time we were performing in the same theater, but we had a few different show days. There was no chance of him coming back to that theater on his day off.

One night, after my shows, I was selling DVDs of that night's live show (the greatest merchandise a hypnotist can sell). Johnathan walked by, grabbed a DVD, and left. On his drive home he called me.

"Do you just want me to tell you you're good?" he asked, then continued in a tired, sarcastic voice, "because OMG you're the best, I love you."

"No, I want your real opinion," I told him.

"Ok," was all he said before he hung up.

Two days later, Johnathan called me over to the house for lunch. In those two days, he had watched that DVD multiple times. He had four pages of single-spaced, double-sided, time-coded notes for me. He tore into every minute and every line in the show, not unkindly, but with the goal of making each moment better and stronger. This is a guy who had toured all over the world, been in all the rooms I wanted to be in, and here he was giving me real-time, moment-to-moment feedback. I could never have paid for that. That was a gift of pure love and friendship. It's also a testament to the person that he was that he would be so generous with his time and his insight.

The second moment when Jonathan taught me an important lesson. It happened as we walked through a mall with him after a show. A mutual person in our world had screwed Johnathan over and he was on a full-scale rant. "Screw this guy. F him. I cannot believe that asshole would do that!" Johnathan was full-on, non-stop ranting when a fan spotted us:

"Oh God, you're *The Amazing Johnathan*!" said the fan.

"Yes. Have you seen the show here in Vegas?" Johnathan replied with that big grin on his face.

Johnathan and the fan talked for less than two minutes. They took a picture together, and the fan bounced away, visibly beaming with joy. Johnathan, with a fresh smile on his face and a happy twinkle in his eye, let out a small sigh, turned back to me, and said: "And ANOTHER thing jerk did..." and went right back to his rant. But for that moment when a fan wanted to say hello, he'd been all smiles and kind words. Johnathan always took the time to give any fan their moment and make them happy. Of all of Johnathan's qualities, that was the most amazing.

The third hugely impactful moment with Johnathan was when I wrote a joke for him. I had watched his show many, many times, and one day I thought of a perfect joke for his set. I didn't know him that well yet, but I knew this joke belonged in the show. I didn't know whether he wanted to hear jokes or ideas from anyone else, so I asked his writing partner, Bruce, and Penny if I should share it with him. They both said yes.

I told Johnathan the joke, his eyes got huge, and he laughed. He'd incorporate it into his show immediately and would later tell me that joke got one of the biggest laughs in his final tour. That was important for me, because I learned that even successful people were glad to take input and ideas. The bigger you are, the more important it is to surround yourself with people who can help you form those ideas. He was gracious in listening and gracious in giving praise to the people who gave him those ideas. It also built up my confidence in my own material that I could do that for him.

Jonathan passed away in 2022. I will forever miss my big brother and treasure every moment we spent together. His wife gave him a memorial that was a true testament to the person, the performer, and the trickster genius he was. His legacy will live on forever.

Chapter 34

The Vegas Adventure Really Begins

"Take my hand
We're off to never-never land." *~Metallica*

I have often told this story about how the start of my Vegas career was meeting someone as I was walking into a restaurant they were walking out of. That story has a lie in it that I want to correct and with their permission, I can tell the real story, from my perspective.

I was walking into a Gamblers Anonymous meeting and saw a guy walking out of an Alcoholics Anonymous wearing a Hypnosis Unleashed t-shirt.

"Great shirt," I said. "Have you seen the show?"

Those were the first words I spoke to Terry Stokes Jr., hypnotist, and son of Terry Stokes Sr. Terry Sr. is a legend in the world of hypnosis. Terry Sr. and Michael Johns were partners in the show *Hypnosis Unleashed* on the Strip.

I must make this extremely clear. I did not meet Jr. because I had fallen, I did not meet him because I was broken. I met him because I wanted to get better, get healthier, and get help. Had I never sought help and therapy, I might have never achieved any of the things that happened next.

Jr. and I began talking, and a friendship formed. We would grab coffee between meetings and chat about different things in our careers. He would occasionally fill in for his dad and I would catch his show. He was funny and great with any crowd. I had never seen Terry Sr. do his show yet. Jr. told me they were having a slow night and I could invite people to come to the show that night to fill up the room. I was glad to bring six people.

Terry Sr. is an amazing performer with one of the smoothest shows I have ever seen or will ever see. He was fantastic. Halfway through the show, he brought Jr. up to do a couple of routines that I had never seen before. As Sr. walked through the audience, he stopped by me and said Jr. had pointed me out and asked if I wanted to do 3-4 minutes. I said sure. Terry introduced me, I did my $100 bill routine and brought Terry back up. After the show, Terry said he liked the routine and invited me to come back the next night if I wanted. I thanked him profusely and calmly walked out the theater door where I screamed my bloody head off!

I had done it. I had performed a routine in a Vegas show!

Sure, it was only three minutes, but it was my three minutes, and I rocked it. My friends and I met for a burger after the show, and I could not stop bouncing around. The adrenaline was rushing through me. I felt like the king of the world. You bet your sweet ass I went back the next night.

At the time, Terry Sr. and Michael Johns would alternate doing the show every few weeks to allow the other free time and the ability to take other gigs. I went to the show every day that week.

Sr. let me do a different routine each night. Every night I asked him question after question, and he graciously answered them all. He told me I was welcome to stick around and hang out at the show anytime. Well, dear readers, by now you know I would never turn that down. I immediately took him up on the offer. The next week I got to meet Michael, who was also a funny, dynamic performer and one of the most stand-up, straightforward people I would ever meet. His show was completely unique from Terry's and a joy to watch. I asked him a lot of questions as well.

For the next six months, I basically became an intern. Any free night I had, I was at the show doing whatever Terry Sr., and Michael needed me to do. I was an onstage assistant, I seated people, took tickets, set up the room—anything they needed. When they wanted to redo their promo, I was on it. I asked for no money. I was just excited to be learning and getting some stage time here and there.

After about six months of this, Terry Sr. and Michael asked me what I wanted for all the help I was supplying the show. I told them exactly what I wanted: the one thing they were not using—their dark night. At the time *Hypnosis Unleashed* show took place six nights a week Friday-Wednesday, and was dark on Thursday. That's what I wanted: for the show to switch to a seven-nights schedule, and for me to perform on Thursdays.

We talked about it over and over for a couple of weeks. We were supposed to have a lunch meeting on Thursday to go over everything. The Wednesday night before I showed up to the show to see Terry Sr. and Michael talking out front. Upon seeing me, Michael turned toward me, looked me in the eye, and said, "You want Thursdays? They're yours."

I want to believe I calmly said thank you as my head and heart exploded inside. My dream had come true. Goals I never thought it possible to achieve as a child considering ending my life—they were all coming true. All the praying, dreaming, and so much challenging work on myself were turning every pie-in-the-sky dream into my reality.

Three weeks from that day, I would be a Vegas Headliner. Oct 14, 2010, everything I had worked for—everything I ever said I wanted in my career—was about to happen.

As I had learned many times over, all the hard work I had done had gotten me here, and now the really hard work was about to begin.

Chapter 35

Why Me?

> ***"I am brave, I am bruised, I am who***
> ***I'm meant to be, this is me."*** *~The Greatest Showman*

This is a big question I've had to ask many times. Why me? Terry and Michael had seen or met about every hypnotist there was. Why would they pick me? Any performer would have taken this opportunity. Why me?

The answer is that I was the first to show up who really wanted to learn. I had the tenacity to come back night after night. I never tried to impress them with what I did, or I told them what I would do differently. I sure as hell never told either of them how or why I was better than them. I was willing to listen and learn.

People ask me how I have grown in my career. The biggest thing is I was willing to learn when others offered to teach me. When I saw that first show at *Hypnosis Unleashed,* I had almost 18 years of performing experience: including eight years' experience traveling the country and five years traveling the world doing high-end shows. But I had no experience performing in Vegas. I was willing to learn, and they were willing to teach.

Whatever they taught me, I put it into action: clothing, manners of presentation, words I was using. I took any critique to heart. Some of it hurt, some of it felt personal, even when it was not. Thankfully working a 12-step program had helped me keep my emotions in check and allowed me to learn rather than becoming defensive. None of their advice was to turn me into them; it was all designed to help me be a better me.

I would have thought any performer would've wanted that kind of valuable input. Sadly, over the years, I would learn that very few people did. I had a hypnotist walk by my showroom while I was selling merch after a show. He put his business card in my hand and told me if the casino wanted a real hypnotist, they could call him. I had a hypnotist who was learning to be a hypnosis instructor walk row to row through my theater before my show showing everyone his demo video on his phone and telling them what he would do in a Vegas show. I had a hypnosis trainer hypnotize his students in front of the line of people waiting to get into my showroom.

I believe people like these are the minorities in performing—people whose egos demand attention no matter what they have to do to get it. Most performers are great. Often, if I have hypnotists in my audience, after the show I will do a Q&A for them in the showroom. I'm glad to answer anything I can because of all the great people who took time for me.

I also showed up and treated it like I was walking into a million-dollar corporate gig every night. I never drank in the showroom; I never brought any drama with me. I treated my business like a business. We all had fun, but I made sure I treated it with the respect it deserved every time I walked in the door. A lot of performers forget that entering a showroom is just like walking into an office. This is where people make their livelihoods. Always treat your business like it is a business.

When Bill has been asked how I've grown my career, he has said, "When Kevin was ready to learn, someone was ready to teach. Kev actively sought out people to learn from. It didn't even matter to him if the person had more or less talent. What was important was whether Kevin felt he could learn from another person's experience."

And that's a lot of the answer to *why me*. Because I was willing to learn from anyone I could. I was willing to put in the work and grow. I was willing to look past being shy or anxious in exchange for learning and growing my career. Without that, it would never have been me.

Chapter 36

Rocking the Harmon

"Hey, now, you're an all-star, get your game on, go play
Hey, now, you're a rock star, get the show on, get paid."
~Smash Mouth

When you are about to start something new, things never seem to go as expected. Nothing went wrong with my first full show for *Hypnosis Unleashed,* but I did get way into my own head.

It was the oddest feeling because something pushed my nervous button, and I defaulted into my corporate show.

I became afraid that if the jokes didn't land, if my personality didn't charm, that I would lose everything at once. My brain went into corporate mode because it was a safe place to go. I had done it so many times it was easy to slip back into.

After the show, Terry and Michael summed up my performance by telling me I was a lot more "leashed" than "unleashed". To their credit, they gave me a mulligan the next night and I hit it out of the park. Now it was time to rock.

Michael and Terry were determined to help me become the best version of myself. Having me do a night a week was not a vacation or easy for them, at least not at first. For about three months, at least one of them was at every show I did. They had to make sure I could keep the standard of the show high. They helped me review and analyze each show to bring out my personality. They had no problem kicking my ass when I needed it and praising me when I deserved it.

Terry even invented a game where we would come up during each other's shows and mess with the volunteers or each other to get us out of our ruts and make us think of new bits. Michael helped me write comedy and was instrumental in helping me reach a new level in launching my personality into everything I did.

It was a non-stop learning experience. I could feel myself getting better. Jokes were getting strong laughs: not smirks and giggles, but full 3–5 second plus laugh breaks. My ability to hypnotize people was getting better, especially because I learned how to work small crowds.

Before I started at the Harmon, I would have told you without any doubt you needed at least fifty people in the audience to do a show. In a smaller showroom, you're going to have nights with 15–20 people. If you bail on a show you booked, not only do you not get paid, but people will stop working with you. You learn to do a show no matter what, or you simply cannot do the job. You learn to make friends with a small audience. You find a way to fill them with confidence that this is going to be a great show—and then it will be.

That is not to say they are all going to be home runs. I'll never forget the worst show I did at the Harmon.

There were nineteen people in the audience. When I was announced, I came out to no applause. Even the crickets were too indifferent to chirp. Every joke in my opening fell flatter than the one before it. It took what felt like an eternity to get seven of them to volunteer, and by some miracle, I hypnotized five out of seven. Things were looking good.

That is, until a woman's head fell to rest on the shoulder of the man next to her, and the man's wife yelled from the crowd, "Don't let that bitch touch you!" SO that woke him up, and we were down to four, plus one gigantic pain in the ass in the audience.

The show was moving, though: Inch by inch, routine by routine I was slowly winning over the audience and I was going to pull a show out of this pile of crap. The final routine was a dance-off, and that went great. But upon ending the routine, one of the volunteers sneezed, and I heard the most visceral reaction from the audience that I have ever heard.

After the show, the volunteer in question admitted to me that he had been on a four-day coke bender. When he sneezed, blood flew out of his nose, down his face and his white (it had to be white right?) shirt. I looked at the audience with all the sincerity I could muster and said, "When I was sixteen, I gave up a job at a pizza place to become an entertainer. If I go back right now, I could still make regional manager by forty."

They are not all going to be home runs. The solution is not always to swing for the fences either. Sometimes you need to look at your audience and quickly figure out how to best play the night. You must know who you are and how to play it.

The Rock once said in an interview, "that the key to playing a successful character is to turn up the volume on aspects of yourself that people like and to turn down everything else." I learned I could move my show between three things that bonded people to me: High Energy, Humor, and Charm. I learned that the shows I loved combined all three. Some nights, the audience wasn't up for high energy, so I would lean into the other two. I learned to evaluate an audience to best deliver what they were in the mood for that night. I didn't blame audiences for not wanting what I was serving; it was my job to give them what they wanted each night.

The Amazing Johnathan was in the bigger showroom attached to ours, and I would often spend time in his dressing room and go out to dinner with him and his crew after the show. Penny and Johnathan became such dear friends. Through them I met Erica Van Lee and Bruce Block, other members of Johnathan's cast. We would have great hours-long dinners after the show. Soon Johnathan's girlfriend, Anastasia—who would become his wife—joined us as well. We would laugh, joke, write material, and have a blast. So many great people joined us at those dinners including the soon-to-be Property Brothers! I met so many great people and had so much fun. I will always treasure those years and hold them close to my heart.

I even got to meet Lady Gaga one night. *The Harmon Theater* became an LGBTQ+ club after the shows were over. One night, a manager asked me to stick around after the show to work security. If you've ever seen me, you would know at once that my body was not designed for security. But the owners had done me enough favors that I wasn't going to say no. Turns out, Lady Gaga was having a show at MGM the next night and had come to do a surprise two-song set for the club to thank her fans. They just wanted me to make sure no one rushed the stage. I met her briefly after the show: she was incredibly sweet and kind to everyone.

A little over a year later, Terry Sr. decided to retire from Vegas, and I took over his days. Erica had left Johnathan's show, and with his blessing, I hired her as our main assistant. Michael and I split weeks and had a wonderful time doing it. Michael really taught me a lot about the business behind Vegas, and he became a big brother to me in so many ways.

There are two incidents I won't ever forget.

The first occurred incredibly early in my stint performing at the Harmon. Two other performers came to watch my show and were rudely on their phones most of the time. About two hours after that show ended, Michael called to tell me all the things he'd heard that I had supposedly said about him—horrible things.

It blew my mind. I had never and would never talk negatively about Michael. After I told him that, he started laughing. He knew I wouldn't, but he also told me to watch my back around other performers because they were apparently hoping to replace me. Very few performers would ever stoop to that level, and I don't know any who succeeded that way.

It was a troubling experience, but it was nothing compared to what happened next.

I was not at this meeting, but I heard all about it from three of the six people who were. They all separately told me the same thing: a manager at the showroom wanted to replace me with another hypnotist so he could make money off him on the side. Michael made it clear that I had earned my spot, and no one was yanking it out from under me; he would shut the show down before he allowed that to happen.

This is the type of friend Michael Johns is: the kind who will defend you when you are not there. The kind who will have your back when no one else is there to protect you. He is honest and true to his word every time. He is the friend you need in your corner if you're going to carry out a goal. He is a brother to me in every meaning of the word. A friend, family, a mentor, and a sounding board. Almost everything I have here in Vegas I have because Michael Johns is my friend, and my friend has never let me fail or fall.

He has also been there to guide me around so many pitfalls in Vegas. He knew why a lot of shows closed and why a lot stayed open. He knew where a lot of performers wasted money and energy. He never told me not to do something; instead, he would tell me the pros and cons based on his own experience. He helped me see things from a business side, not an ego side. He would be there as that big brother to guide me when otherwise I would have failed.

As rooms in Vegas do, the Harmon was closing. Michael also decided it was time for him to retire from Vegas shows, but he gave me his blessing to use the name *Hypnosis Unleashed* going forward. If it were going to continue, it would have to continue on my shoulders. Thankfully, Michael would still be around to help me and guide me. His advice was always important to me. He would tell me mistakes he made in the business of Vegas, saving me a lot of trouble. He helped me to avoid mistakes and rise to success.

And I would. But first I had to find a room.

Chapter 37

Love That Owl

"Coming from afar

Reaching for the stars." *~Pras*

It's much easier to get a showroom in Vegas when you already have a room in Vegas, so I hit the pavement, looking at every possible spot: banquet rooms, retail space, other showrooms with time slots available. I looked everywhere.

This is harder than it might sound. To a tourist, Vegas seems to have a *lot* of casinos. The Vegas Strip gives the appearance of dozens of casinos stacked next to one another. In reality, there are about six. MGM owns about a third of the Strip and Caesar's owns another third. Neither of them wanted a hypnosis show. That left me with only about five casinos. Most of them either didn't have anything like a showroom or didn't want to lose meeting space to create a showroom. Others had one major show and didn't want another show to compete with that. Some were just—in my opinion—out of their minds.

It works like this: Most venues will either charge you rent or a percentage of ticket sales. On top of that, some venues demand thousands of dollars a week for advertising. Others will charge you for eight hours of union labor to put on your seventy-five-minute show. Then they'll add box office fees and other costs. Combined, these fees can make running a show almost impossible.

I had the idea that Hooters Casino would be a great fit for me, but I couldn't get a call back from them. It was an excellent location and had an unused showroom. After a number of unanswered calls over the course of a month, I left a final message with the general manager:

"I really want to do business with your casino," I said. "Unfortunately, no one will call me back!"

It worked! I got a call back. I made my pitch to the GM. He was very interested. It was time to talk business.

Thankfully, the *Hypnosis Unleashed* brand was already known in Vegas, so the meeting was simple and went perfectly. They were glad to have a known show with solid reviews and a following coming in. Hooters would be the new home of *Hypnosis Unleashed starring Kevin Lepine*. To put a cherry on top, the ticket brokers stayed with me and were ready to start selling the show as soon as I had the venue.

With forty-five days from the Harmon closing to the show opening at Hooters, I got to work. I opened a crowdfunding campaign online to help me spread the news. It also helped spread the love. Everyone who had something to offer did. People from all chapters of my past joined in to donate and spread the word. Friends showed up to help build out the room. Artist friends created an entirely new poster and advertising look. Michael Johns met ticket brokers with me to offer advice on which brokers I needed on my side and what I would need to open.

Even the other performing hypnotists jumped in to help. Marc Savard, who had a show at the V Theater, sent me a wonderful gift basket and offered advice and support. Anthony Cools came by to see the room, and not only did he make suggestions, but he also gave me a backdrop that made it look so much better.

Pegasus Entertainment really blew me away. I've talked about the great relationship I shared with David and Kevin in Detroit. Now I needed a lot of things: most importantly, curtains. A lot of curtains. Front stage, side stage, entryway, and wall-covering drapery. I talked with them about what I needed and how much so they could get a quote together for me. I was hoping they had some used stuff we could make do with to keep the budget together.

A week later, I got the call to go to Hooters to sign for a delivery. Pegasus had sent all the curtains I needed with no bill, just a letter from David and Kevin congratulating me on the deal. I sat surrounded by boxes, smiling, and crying.

There are people who love to be discouraging to others. The sharks told me many negative things: that my show would never last, that I would never make it, that I didn't deserve the opportunity. I received all levels of hate from sharks in my industry. But I received so much more love that the hate was never worth looking at. So many people were part of my school of fish and wanted to lift me up. No hatred, no sharks, could take me down. My community was too strong for me to even hear them. I was ready to swim.

My show opened on October 11, 2012 (10-11-12) to a full room. I couldn't believe it. The show went off perfectly. Part of me is always just pessimistic enough to believe nothing will happen until it does. Having the show open successfully was awesome. We had great nights, and we had hard nights. Every night was an adventure because it was mine. My dream, my shoulders, my triumphs, and my disappointments.

Management told me they really liked my show, but more importantly, they found me easy to work with and liked collaborating with me. I'm glad they liked me because upper management was about to change.

For whatever reason, the hotel company decided it needed to make a change about five months after I started performing there. This is scary because you never know if the new management will want to keep you.

Thankfully, they did. I had a great meeting with the new team soon after they came in. They generously offered to help me by picking up some of my expenses and increasing my advertising. I was thrilled. On top of that, they were bringing in "Purple Reign," a Prince tribute band.

So not only was Hooters putting more money into the showroom, but they were also bringing in an act that put more eyes on my shows. The biggest bonus is that everyone in "Purple Reign" from top to bottom were great guys who wanted everyone around them to be better. Jason, who performs as Prince, was a leader on fire. He'd surrounded himself with amazing musicians who were fantastically driven people. Jason gave me show and music ideas. He did a photoshoot for me and created my next level of promo material. When my sound guy was unavailable, one of his would step in. His show manager—also named Kevin—and I would work together to make the transition between our shows seamless. Audiences had no idea that the hypnosis show had ended, and the band was up in running in under twenty minutes!

I know I say this often, but most people at the top of their field know there is always more room at the top. The number of fantastic people I have met in show business outnumber the shitheads ten to one. It brings tears to my eyes when I look back on all the people who have helped me to grow repeatedly.

My good thing had gotten so much better.

Chapter 38

Hooters is Going Great and *Best of Vegas*

> ***"So, bring your good times and your laughter too***
> ***We gonna celebrate your party with you, come on."***
> *~Kool & The Gang*

In 2013, Mike Metcalf was the new Hooters GM, and he also became a great friend who took the time to listen to my ideas about the show. I didn't want to waste his time, so I was careful about which ideas I brought him. We also spent time together and talked as friends (and still do to this day).

But once again, things had changed, and the hotel was going on the market. *Purple Reign* and I were given ninety days. It was a generous deal considering the standard thirty days or the *get out now* most casinos would give you. After that meeting, Mike called me in and made me an offer: They planned to revert my showroom to (more profitable) meeting space and reopen the main showroom for me. They loved *Purple Reign*, but since I was basically an established one-person show, I was easier to keep than let go. He would give me a new contract with the understanding that the contract could terminate at any time if the hotel sold. That six-month contract turned into over two years.

I won my first *Best of Vegas: Best Hypnotist Award* while at Hooters. I was so grateful. Not only was my show surviving in Vegas, but I was thriving. I also won the *Reader's Choice Best of Vegas Award* during that time. I felt like I earned it and that I belonged. I had seen the online sharks predicting that I would fail, only to have a school of fish buoy me up and help build on my success each year. It was not up to the naysayers to direct my career—it was up to me and all the people who supported me and came to the show. My school of fish had expanded again and again and helped me achieve, even exceed, my dreams.

I also began to teach a hypnosis course with Bill. He was still living in New Orleans running his own successful practice as a Licensed Social Worker (L.C.S.W). We decided to teach the course together, as it would be fun and give us an excuse to hang out more. With his grounding in clinical hypnosis as part of his practice and mine in stage hypnosis, we could offer a course that would prepare students to get out there and perform safely. I am proud of the students we taught, and some of them are doing wonderful things with their own shows now.

That was not the best thing to happen while at Hooters though.

Chapter 39

The Best Thing to Ever Happen to Me

"Here comes the sun, and I say,

It's all right." *~The Beatles*

Erica Van Lee was my main assistant in 2012. She would seat guests and keep volunteers safe. Her years working for *The Amazing Johnathan* made my show simple by comparison. Erica worked a lot of great gigs and often needed time off, so we decided to hire two new assistants: Erin and Emily. All three "E's" were fantastic at their jobs.

Emily, however, changed my life and became the best thing to ever happen to me.

The first time I saw Emily, she was performing in a poorly produced burlesque as M.C. and hostess. She was good, but the show was bad. My friend Bizarro, who was also performing, had invited me to come and watch how much of a train wreck it was.

Emily is also the understudy lead in the show *Marriage Can Be Murder*, an extremely popular dinner theater show in Vegas. She had a reputation for having a quick wit and being amazingly easy to work with. Multiple people I respected told me Emily would be perfect for *Hypnosis Unleashed*, so I set up an interview. She came to the casino to watch the show and to interview with Erica and me. Erica had known her from other events and was excited to bring her on board. I was happy that she had worked with another hypnotist and was familiar with what I needed. We decided to give her a shot.

Training Emily was straightforward, as she had a lot of stage experience and knew how to ingratiate herself with an audience. Audience members really liked her. Emily thought she was miscast because she wasn't using her comedy skills. While gorgeous, she did not think the role of a beautiful assistant worked for her.

Five minutes before the doors opened on Emily's very first show, the zipper on the back of her dress split. She was almost in tears. I handed her a t-shirt and she quickly made it into an impromptu top for the dress. She would later write on Facebook that it was nice to be part of a show where management wanted everyone to keep their clothes on.

One of Erica's jobs was to watch the other assistants to evaluate their work and to suggest improvements where she could. When Erica called Emily to tell her she was coming in to watch, Emily thought she was being fired.

"Erica, you don't have to be nice," Emily said. "Sometimes things don't work out. If you're going to fire me, you can do it over the phone."

Emily was doing well, but she felt that I didn't like working with her. Erica told her nothing was further from the truth, and when I found out, I told Emily how well she was doing. The three of us would laugh about this time and again. Especially as Emily and I got closer.

The hypnosis was foreign to her, but getting the crowd to like her in the right way was second nature. I need women to feel comfortable around my assistant, and I need women to feel comfortable sending their significant others up next to her. I also need guys to think she is friendly without feeling they should be hitting on her. I have no idea how to teach these skills at all. Emily has them ten times over.

What I did not know was that Emily's marriage was ending. Emily and I worked together for almost a year before we really started talking personally. Even those conversations were mostly professional. She was working on stand-up and her own performances, and I would watch and give her notes. Emily was looking to get out of the house more, and I had invites to a lot of the same events she ended up at. Slowly, very slowly, it went from Emily spending time together with all of us to Emily and me spending time together, just us, more and more. Then one night, we went down to Fremont Street, and she found $50 lying on the ground. (This is an amazing side talent of hers; I don't know how she does it, but she finds money a lot). We ended up at the pool and shark tank at the Golden Nugget. It was quiet, we were alone, and everything was perfect when we kissed for the first time.

I need to make a lot clear, here. Emily was in the process of the divorce and getting a place alone. Her marriage was over before I came into the picture. She did not leave anyone for me, I did not take her from anyone. She was starting a new life and that kiss was a part of it. While we were rarely far from each other, I was a little emotionally hesitant about her. She was great, but also starting a new life. I didn't know if she wanted to be in a relationship. I did not know if she was sure about her decisions. I knew I cared for her and had love in my heart for her. I just didn't know if she knew what she wanted. And I wouldn't know until the night when her ex-husband jumped me.

I know how weird that sounds. I had put together a charity event for a great cause in Vegas and was lucky to fill the bill with some great family performers. I acted as the emcee. Well, Emily's ex showed up, stalked me till he found me alone, called my name, and when I turned, he punched me then poked me in the eye. I barely flinched. I say that not to sound tough. I really think I was just too confused and shocked in that second. When I did not go down, he took off. Witnesses saw the attack and called the police. I quickly cleaned up since I was going on stage in three minutes.

We talked to the police in between acts. As the show ended, the police had one final question for Emily: Did she want to file charges? This was a big moment; in many earlier relationships, when a girlfriend had to make a stand and say they were on my side, they had faltered.

Emily didn't flinch or falter for a second before telling them:

"Hell yes, I do!" All while wearing her pink fluffy clown costume for the show.

In that moment, I knew I was in love with her, clown suit and all. When she could have waffled or made excuses or even decided this was all too much, she wanted to stand up next to me. I have never left her side since, and I never will.

Every night in the show, and any time people ask about our relationship, I always say, "She makes my life better and easier by being in it." That is the truth. I have never had someone enter my life and make it simpler. She does not bring drama; she brings a grounded sense of reality. She does not bring arguments, she brings discussion. She does not bring games; she brings honesty and compassion. When she makes a decision, she thinks first about how it will affect everyone around her. I am beyond lucky to have her in my life, and I will never forget that.

When you enter a relationship with someone, you also enter a relationship with their family. I did not understand Emily's family for a long time. They build each other up with words and actions of love and respect. They go out of their way to help each other and help each other to grow. It took me a while to understand it was not bullshit. It is an absolutely loving family that wants the best for each other. That they would extend that love to me is such a wonderful gift. I am glad they are a part of my life and my heart.

Chapter 40

Binion's

"So go downtown, things'll be great when you're Downtown, don't wait a minute more Downtown,

Everything's waiting for you." *~Petula Clark*

After multiple extensions, Hooters finally sold to another company. Thankfully, Mike got them to honor my contract, which gave me four months to find a new room. The search began.

Now that the show had been running under my own name, I had a bit more of a reputation. This made getting meetings with entertainment directors a bit easier. It also made me wiser in terms of deals I would and would not accept.

As I've mentioned, a lot of Vegas shows have failed. Shows open and close here constantly. A major factor in whether a show will be successful is the deal. Some venues charge so much you are almost destined to fail. I had one offer that asked for $5,000 a week in rent, $5,000 a week in advertising, an $8.95 box office fee on every ticket (including comps), 10% of the box office gross and merchandise sales, plus they wanted to charge me for four hours of union staff. All this for a fifty-five-minute time slot in an off-strip property in a tiny showroom. I would have had to sell out every night to break even. Deals like that are a nonstarter.

The other deal I wanted to avoid is the dreaded *room that can lead to another room* deal. I see this one fail here all the time: A show takes a bad deal in a room that cannot generate an audience. The room may not have the support of a casino or hotel. It may not be visible or have walking traffic to spur interest in the show. But performers take the room all in hopes that by having a gig in town they can quickly get a better showroom. The truth is, if the better showroom wanted you, they would have made you an offer. Entertainment directors are too busy with their shows to see yours. It really holds you back instead of moving forward. Anytime you are looking at getting a showroom, the goal is not to move somewhere better. The goal is to make the room you are in the best it can be.

Through a great friend of mine, I had made a friend in Glenn, the casino manager for Binion's Gambling Hall on Fremont Street in Downtown Vegas. We had lunch and discussed looking for a new room. Binion's had just had a museum close in their complex, so there was space available. I always loved Fremont Street—I love Vegas history, and it all started downtown. The stories and happenings at Binion's are Vegas legend. Glenn, along with the executive assistant, Michele, championed bringing me over.

Meeting with everyone at Binion's was a fantasy come true. The deal was great, but the people were far better. Every deal is only as good as the people making it, and the people are amazing. This is a privately run business that was designed with the customers in mind. Everyone from the owner to the GM and managers are all there with the goal of making Binion's the best experience possible. Not only did they want my show, but they also wanted my show to succeed.

I knew I had found a new home.

Chapter 41

My 40th Birthday Present

> ***"Wise men say only fools rush in,***
>
> ***But I can't help falling in love with you."*** ~ *Elvis Presley*

Emily and I were making all the plans for Binion's while finishing our contract at Hooters. We even had a vacation planned. We had a show the night before our vacation, and after the show had an appointment to meet Bizzaro on Fremont Street to discuss promotional materials. Emily did not want to go, as we needed to eat and finish packing, but I insisted this was important.

After looking at the promo positions at Binion's with Bizzaro and his wife Liz, I took the four of us to the pool at the Golden Nugget to show them all a poster I wanted them to see.

This was June 21, 2015, on the eve of my 40th birthday. That night I said something I had never said in my life and did something I will never do again: I got down on one knee and asked Emily to marry me.

Very few people knew this was going to happen! I kept the circle small so it would be a surprise. Biz and Liz knew—that's why they were there. Emily's stepfather knew, as I had called him a few days before to ask his permission. He was the only one to make me nervous when he asked me if I was sure she would say yes. I was pretty sure.

There is a great moment in the video when Emily turns around to see me on one knee with the ring. She slowly set down a bottle of water she'd been holding in one hand and then threw her purse from the other. She convinced me it was a surprise by pointing out her nails were not done. She said yes!

This woman who made every part of my life better was going to be my wife! In the next few months, Emily and I bought a house, built a showroom, ended one contract to start another, and began planning a wedding. We like to keep things calm.

When the folks at Binion's saw the engagement video, they offered us a fantastic opportunity to get married there. On October 15, 2016, Binion's threw us a wedding I can never thank them enough for. We got married on the pool deck surrounded by loved ones and threw a joyous dinner party in the meeting room. Binion's kitchen staff outdid themselves with amazing food, and so many of our friends pitched in to make it unforgettable.

Emily and I often say we had the easiest wedding of all time because so many of our friends made it perfect. Our friend Tawney Bubbles, the greatest balloon decorator of all time, made the room look amazing and created 10-foot-tall balloon figures of us. Steve Falcon ran all our sound and helped keep things running on time. Shea Arender found the band for us, emceed the reception to keep everything moving, and most importantly sang our first dance song "Can't Help Falling in Love." All our friends and family came together to make it so perfect. Looking at my friends Don and Bill as my best man and officiant, respectively, made me feel so confident. To see my groomsmen Michael Johns, Alex Getz, Bizzaro, Amazing Johnathan, WWE Superstar Sinn Bodhi, and Emily's brother Josh standing there, I knew everything was perfect. I will also always say, my bride was more beautiful and more sparkly than your bride. While one of those statements may be my opinion, the other is fact!

I could look around and see and feel all the fish who swam with me to get me here—this school of fish of mine was amazing. To have friends and family all coming together to share in the love. We have family members and friends on every end of every belief possible, yet no one found differences, just togetherness. I had come a long way professionally from doing birthday parties in Detroit. I had grown as a person to become someone who could share in love with someone as amazing as Emily.

Chapter 42

Building the Showroom

"Whatever it takes

Yeah, take me to the top I'm ready for

Whatever it takes

'Cause I love the adrenaline in my veins." *~Imagine Dragons*

I was able to build out the space in the old museum and call it *The Lepine-Goldman Theater*. I love that it would stand for my family as well as my show. Once again so many people helped me which is great because on the first day of construction, I got food poisoning and could not do anything.

It was not the greatest showroom in Vegas, but we built it with love and the audience in mind: a 99-seat theater that had wall-to-wall postering advertising the show and not a bad seat in the house. We had an exciting time at Binion's. While my mom and dad could not make it out to the opening, Robin Leach did. My mom used to watch his show, *Lifestyles of the Rich and Famous* every week, so getting a picture of her son with Robin really let her feel like I'd made it.

Growing a new showroom is difficult, but Binion's did everything they could to help us. They allowed us to put promo anywhere there was space in the complex. I started a pocket magazine that they put everywhere as well. Inch by inch we built it, and the show grew. We were getting amazing responses from the crowds and making it happen. Emily had a great schedule; she was in another show two casinos down from ours. She became known as the 8 o'clock running girl as she would go from one show to the other. What made it so wonderful was that Emily and I did it together.

One of the most amazing things about achieving my dream is that I get to enjoy living it with the woman of my dreams. We know each other and trust each other on stage. We would rather talk things out than argue, and we both want to help each other realize our dreams. Emily came up with the idea of learning to play violin and using it in the show. She was worried I would think wanting to learn an instrument was silly. I decided I would take piano lessons and we could grow together. Everything we do, we do together, and it makes everything work.

I also started doing more for the hypnosis community. In 2016 I was honored to perform for *Hypno-Thoughts* and be a guest speaker at multiple conventions. Emily and I also hosted our own conventions and workshops. I still learn constantly, and being surrounded by other successful people and listening to their journey still helps me to grow.

I also made it a policy to take time to talk with performers when they come to the show. I am always glad to sit and chat, to go over what I do or why I do it. So many people have helped me. I feel a responsibility to give back. I love teaching hypnosis courses and sharing my stories with others.

Things at Binion's got even better when Binion's re-opened The Hotel Apache, known as *Vegas' Most Haunted Hotel*. Having guests staying at the casino helped to increase business for us a lot. I was even asked to bring back my séance recreation.

This gave Emily and me another project to work on together, and it required us to hire some great performers. The séance recreation was split into two parts: a twenty-minute tour through the hotel, and an hour in a hidden area of the hotel's past. The ambiance and real-life stories of that area gave it a vibe that was unlike anything else.

Along with the hotel re-opening, Binion's had an even bigger surprise for us. They would build us a new showroom! This showroom would be downstairs, the site of Benny Binion's original steakhouse. This room was gorgeous. The classic Vegas look and gorgeously restored original wood made the Apache showroom the most beautiful room I'd had the privilege of performing in. The original wooden staircase led to a stained-glass lobby and into an intimate ninety-seat room that felt like Sinatra would be taking the stage. The room was perfect.

By Feb of 2020, I knew nothing could stop us or hold us back. Then March of 2020 came, and the world shut down.

Chapter 43

Lockdown

> ***"It's the end of the world***
>
> ***As we know it,***
>
> ***And I feel fine."*** *~R.E.M.*

We came down with COVID early on into the lockdown. Emily and I both had horrible symptoms. Mine got worse, and I ended up in the hospital for about 3 days. I was too tired to remember most of it. I do remember there was talk of stepping up my oxygen to another level when, thank God, I started to improve. Even after leaving the hospital, it would be a couple of weeks before I felt human again.

I can't tell you how awful the lockdown was for Emily and me because it really was not. Emily got an online teaching assistant job, and I was teaching hypnosis to chiropractors. We got by and took time for each other. We made a habit of daily walks and planning what we wanted to do when the world reopened. We rescued a bunny. We found a way to enjoy each day. We took time and had dinner with friends. We cooked more and just enjoyed being with each other. More than ever before we started to understand what we did and did not want out of day-to-day life.

Emily really showed me the value of slowing down. She showed me that I was always worried about taking any time off, as though it meant the world would end. Well, the world was on pause, and it had nothing to do with my show. We knew when we came back it would be five nights a week instead of six. We decided we really wanted to travel more, and that we would take two weeks off to enjoy somewhere we had not been.

All the while, we waited to hear when our show would re-open. At that moment, no one knew when, or even if, shows would be coming back. Would performers be allowed to use audience volunteers if the show did open? Would there be live entertainment anymore?

We got the best news possible.

Chapter 44

The Four Queens

"You can get it if you really want
But you must try, try, and try, try, and try
***You'll succeed at last."** ~Jimmy Cliff*

Binion's and the Four Queens are owned by the same company. Mike Hammer has been the 7 p.m. comedy and magic show at the Four Queens for many years. Mike and I had been friends for a while before this. When I opened inside Binion's, the casino checked with Mike to make sure it was not a conflict for him, as he was at the Four Queens. Mike was thrilled for me, and we always kept communications open.

Besides his show he also produced another show at 9 p.m. inside the Four Queens. With the lockdown ending not only did the casino not want to run a showroom at Binion's and the Four Queens, but Mike was no longer producing the other show. Mike came up with the idea of *Hypnosis Unleashed* taking the 9 p.m. slot.

This was huge for us. Moving to the Four Queens meant a bigger showroom, a bigger hotel, and more advertising. The Four Queens was thrilled to help promote us in ways I had never even thought of. They were offering me a huge promotion that I was so excited to take, and Mike went beyond on so many levels as well.

Once this idea became reality, Mike and I went to dinner. There was never a moment of conflict or one-upmanship. It was just two people who wanted the best for the showroom and the shows. We started looking at who had what and what we could combine to make it even better. Anything either of us could do to help the other, we did it.

The way Mike, Emily, and I came together made it easy for us to become great friends. All we wanted was the best for each other. Oddly enough, we even discovered Mike and Emily were cousins through marriage. I can't explain how great it is to be around people who will build you up. A lot of performers are insecure and threatened by others. Successful performers only want success for others. Thankfully, Mike is not only a successful performer but a great comedian and person.

Mike also became a director for me. He took time to watch my show much like Johnathan had all those years before. Mike helped me cut the extra words out of my show to improve my timing. He helped me get rid of unnecessary blabbering and get to the point. He helped me make the jokes tighter and the routines funnier. He did it all with the idea of wanting to help make my show stronger.

He didn't need to take the time. He could have just ignored me. He had no investment other than friendship, but that made him want to help—and help it has. My show is better and more efficient from laugh to laugh. It is more fun for the audience, and it is more fun for Emily and me. We have a great staff, a great show, a great show leading into ours in a great property that wants us to succeed.

Chapter 45

The Most Important People in the Show

"Hey, don't write yourself off yet

It's only in your head, you feel left out

Or looked down on." *~Jimmy Eat World*

I have talked about everyone else except the most important people in a hypnosis show: the volunteers. Without audience members volunteering every night, I wouldn't have a show. Treating them well is my main goal. Watching them has created so many ideas for so many of the routines I love to do.

Yes, it is funny to watch people grabbing for napkins they believe are hundred-dollar bills. You can't help but laugh when big guys think they are giving birth, or a group of volunteers become showgirls. But there is so much more to it than that. The volunteers also get to feel empowered. I often hear from my volunteers,

"I didn't think I could ever do that!"

They're not talking about being hypnotized, but about even getting up on stage. By nature, most of my people are very shy in their day-to-day life. I admire their courage even choosing to volunteer. Once under, they become amazing, outgoing, and my superstars for the evening's show. Many had never believed that they could cut loose in front of a group of people. Getting hypnotized opens their eyes to a world of new possibilities.

Each volunteer takes on the fear of being watched in public, and ultimately they feel like superstars for doing it. They realize that they can get in front of a crowd without panicking. If you can be hypnotized to dance onstage or speak like you just arrived from Mars, you have a new feeling of confidence. Getting up and speaking at work or to a professional is no longer a daunting feeling.

So many people have told me how participating in my show increased their confidence; how they were able to let go of fears and phobias because they realized what they could do after being hypnotized.

Yes, it is funny to watch a grown man become a pop princess while hypnotized. It is funny to watch him sing and dance his heart out to the music. But it is empowering when we are laughing *with* him during his performance. As funny as it is, imagine a moment in your life when you felt shy. Remember a time when you did not want to deliver a speech and how it made you feel. Then imagine the great feeling a person has after they not only survived something they thought was impossible for them but received a standing ovation while doing it.

I have watched volunteers on stage go from nervous to confident public speakers. I've watched after shows as timid participants were praised by family, friends, and strangers for being so outgoing.

I once had a woman start sneezing because she believed the stuffed cat she was holding was real. I told her at that moment she was not allergic anymore and she stopped sneezing. She emailed three weeks later to tell me her allergies were totally gone!

My favorite, though, is from a routine onstage I will do with spouses. I'll have the husband or wife hypnotized onstage with the spouse watching in the audience. Especially when it is an older couple, I will bring the spouse from the audience to the stage.

"What's your favorite color?" I ask the unhypnotized spouse.

"Red (or another color)," they will reply.

"Whenever you are onstage and say the color red, your spouse will slowly saunter over and give you the biggest, most passionate kiss of all time," I tell the hypnotized spouse.

As soon as the unhypnotized spouse says the color, it happens. A glorious exclamation of love. It is funny but also amazing to watch love light up in a person's eyes as they go to kiss their loved ones. I will usually leave that color *activated* for the rest of the night for the couple to enjoy. The suggestion is gone by the end of the night, with one fantastic exception.

I had a couple who had been married for almost thirty years. I must be honest, the kiss the husband put on his wife's lips that night was inspiring! Nine months later they came back to the show and the color was still working! In their day-to-day life, this couple was very reserved. They both came from a background that looked down on public displays of affection. That color gave them the permission they had wanted their entire lives. It gave them not only the joy of being able to express their love in that way but a safe way to also say they wanted it.

I love watching people achieve things when the mental blocks they have set up are removed. I love seeing love and joy spread across their faces. I love being able to use my talents to not only make people laugh but to see how much more they can do in their lives. Hypnosis has given me the ability to help others get rid of their sharks. I love helping them do that.

Chapter 46

Success

"Mr. Wonka: Don't forget what happened to

the man who suddenly got everything he wanted.

Charlie Bucket: What happened?

Mr. Wonka: He lived happily ever after." *~Willy Wonka*

I feel like we are succeeding. Not only is the show a success, but our audiences are growing. Most of the success comes from feeling so fulfilled. Not only do I get to live my dream, but Emily is also by my side, making it better. I am performing in a room with friends and management who want us to succeed. We have friends and family that support our dreams and goals.

Love is the greatest feeling of success!

You can make all the money in the world and be unhappy. The goal cannot just be about the money, it must be about what you really want to do. If you are fulfilled inside, you will always make enough. If you feel unfulfilled or empty inside, no money will ever be enough to fill the hole. It is hard to look inside to figure out what you really want, and that is different for everyone.

We all have different versions of happiness. I know the idea of going onstage nightly and doing what I do is some people's definition of hell. I know that living in Las Vegas is not for everyone.

But for me, it has been amazing. This was where I wanted to be. Here in Las Vegas, I get to live the professional life I always dreamed of. I loved my time on the road, but I always wanted my own show in my own showroom. Las Vegas has given me that.

I know that all of us need to find the unique things we want to be happy. I have them. The boy who thought he had nothing became the man who has everything.

I look at my school of fish in the showroom and it fills me with joy. I get to live my dream with the woman of my dreams by my side. I get to do it in a venue filled with people who want me to succeed. I meet people every night who thank me for the experience of coming to the show, and I want to thank each of them for being a part of it all. But then that view grows. I see the community in Vegas that has always supported me, and the friendships that help me enjoy every day, and suddenly that school of fish is much bigger.

As I look back, I see the friends who have stayed with me throughout all the years. All the friends who have always been there with a positive word to build me up when I needed it. The ones who have provided a shoulder to cry on and the ones who have been there to celebrate the victories with me. The ones who I know build me up even when I am not around. As long as I have those fish in my life, there is no room for sharks to get near me.

I see how my family has grown, getting bigger and filled with love. I see the love and pride in my parents' eyes. To see the pride and love in Howard and Lori's eyes is a gift I do not know how to say thank you for. All my siblings fill me with joy and happiness. To have ten siblings in my life is incredible. That all of them are so unique is a joy to learn from. I see various parts of myself in them as well as their individuality. It is an incredible feeling to have family that gives me strength, confidence, and love.

I see different versions of myself; the child who was hurt, the kid who was abused, the teen first making friends, the performer, the broken, and the healthy. I see all the love I am given by so many. I know how big my school of fish is.

I know that school keeps growing and teaching me. They have all taught me to have love for myself. To love and cherish the person I am, and to want to share that love. I know there is no shark powerful enough to take that love away. Good times do not always last, but good people do. I am so fortunate to have so many good people in my life. To have a community that I made by reaching out.

It can be scary; not everyone you reach out to will reach back in the ways you want. The ones who do, the ones who really make themselves there for you, that is your community. I know every day will have challenges and joys. It is so much easier to see the joys. I get to overcome the challenges knowing how many people are swimming with me. I get to look at my school of fish and feel able to achieve.

I am almost fifty years old and finally ready to live each and every day.

Anti-Bullying Resources

This book is not intended to provide medical or mental health advice, diagnosis, or treatment. I survived bullying and abuse. I have thrived, I believe you can too! If you are being bullied, know it truly can get better. It might seem dark and depressing, but you too can overcome it. Feel free to reach out to the resources that William listed resources in the Foreword, and I have added some additional ones here. You are stronger and more powerful than you think! Success and happiness are the best forms of revenge! All my best to you, ***Kevin***

<u>Anti-Bullying Resources</u>

- www.cfchildren.org/resources/bullying-prevention-resources
- www.stopbullying.gov
- www.schoolsafety.gov/bullying-and-cyberbullying
- www.learningforjustice.org/professional-development/bullying-help-resources-and-partners
- www.pacer.org/bullying/info/sites-for-kids-and-teens.asp
- https://anti-bullyingalliance.org.uk/anti-bullying-week-2023-make-noise-about-bullying/school-resources
- www.parentcenterhub.org/bullying/
- www.antibullying.eu/about_bullying
- http://enable.eun.org/

If you or someone you know has a gambling problem reach out to:

- www.gamblersanonymous.org

Free Resources

Thank you for purchasing my book. Your support means the world to me. There is exclusive bonus content available to you for absolutely free! These chapters were cut from the book and contain valuable insights on how to get a show in Vegas and my personal thoughts on growing a show.

You can access these chapters by visiting:

HypnosisUnleashed.com/bookoffer

As an added bonus, you have the opportunity to receive a free autographed 6x9 postcard of the book cover. This postcard is only available while supplies last, so act fast and claim your free postcard today.

All my best,

Kevin

Ordering Information

For individual worldwide copies of this book:

Amazon.com

(Or the Amazon website specific to your country)

Case-lot orders for resale, educational, and non-profit purposes, contact your local book wholesaler through Ingram or Baker & Taylor. You may also inquire at:

HypnosisUnleashed.com

For speaking/training opportunities from Kevin:

HypnosisUnleashed.com

www.ingramcontent.com/pod-product-compliance
Lightning Source LLC
Chambersburg PA
CBHW032042090426
42744CB00004B/90